JUST COHABITING?

JUST COHABITING?

*The Church, Sex and
Getting Married*

DUNCAN DORMOR

DARTON · LONGMAN + TODD

First published in 2004 by
Darton, Longman and Todd Ltd
1 Spencer Court
140–142 Wandsworth High Street
London SW18 4JJ

ISBN 0–232–52484–X

A catalogue record for this book is available from the British Library.

Designed by Sandie Boccacci
Phototypeset in 10/14pt Melior
by Intype Libra Ltd
Printed and bound in Great Britain by
Page Bros, Norwich, Norfolk

To Catherine, naturally

CONTENTS

ACKNOWLEDGEMENTS

My thanks go first of all to the couples who have shared something of their lives with me in preparation for their wedding day; to the Revd Dr Jeremy Worthen and Philip Hadridge for their encouragement and critical comments on an earlier draft; to Dr Jack Dominian and Penny Mansfield for deepening my interest in the subject matter of this book and for the three delightful years I spent working for the research charity, One plus One: Marriage and Partnership Research. I am also deeply grateful to Brendan Walsh and his team at DLT for their patience, but most especially to Catherine who had to exercise the same virtue even more frequently.

Some of the material in this book, especially in Chapter 6, is reproduced from ' "Come Live with Me and Be My Love": Marriage, Cohabitation and the Church' from *Anglicanism: The Answer to Modernity*, eds Duncan Dormor, Jack McDonald and Jeremy Caddick (London: Continuum, 2003). Throughout this book 'Church' is used to refer to the Church of England, unless stated otherwise.

The Scripture quotations are taken from the *Revised Standard Version*.

CHAPTER ONE

Facing the challenge

'Church must face trend of living together.' This challenge was issued in the form of a front page headline of *The Church of England Newspaper* of 14 February 1992,[1] and was followed three years later by a working party of the Church's Board of Social Responsibility that made a real contribution to the discussion of cohabitation in its publication *Something to Celebrate*. This report spoke of cohabitation as a 'step along the way' to marriage and argued that the popularity of cohabitation was:

> an opportunity and a challenge to the Church to articulate its doctrine of marriage in ways so compelling, and to engage in a practice of marriage so life-enhancing, that the institution of marriage regains its centrality.[2]

Sadly there has been little subsequent evidence for such articulation and engagement. Indeed the wide-ranging and realistic picture of contemporary family life painted in the report received a very rough ride in certain quarters,[3] not least in General Synod, which may well account for the subsequent timidity of the Church of England in addressing the subject.

Four years on, *Marriage*,[4] a teaching document from the House of Bishops was published. Whilst there is much to commend in it, it is very much a document in the 'declamatory' style, blissfully unaware, or perhaps uninterested in, the history of marriage or the changing social context in which marriages are made today. Two central assertions in this document, which will come in for some critical scrutiny in this book, seem particularly distant from the world in which most of us live. First, that 'sexual intercourse, as an expression of faithful intimacy, properly belongs with marriage *exclusively*.'[5] Second, that pre-marital cohabitation as a 'route of approaching marriage is exposed to uncertainties and tensions and is not to be recommended'.[6]

As should be abundantly clear, there has been a complete collapse in the plausibility of religiously based prohibitions on pre-marital sexual expression within Western society over the last thirty years. According to the most reliable available information, less than 1 per cent of people marrying are virgins, which given that the average age at first marriage is now around 30 years is perhaps unsurprising. How has this situation arisen? In some people's eyes, the answer is fairly simple: society is in moral decline and changes in sexual behaviour are the clearest indication of the development of a 'permissive' culture which, to be blunt, lacks discipline. In this account, however it is dressed up, cohabitation is 'living in sin': it represents a dilution of the gold standard of traditional Christian morality and the best way forward is to turn back the clock – somehow.

In this book, I shall argue that the development of widespread cohabitation[7] in Western society cannot be understood without a more profound consideration of the connection between sexuality and procreation, and the way in which this has been radically altered by the development of new contraceptive methods (see especially Chapter 4). Reliable, efficient contraception is part of the 'givenness' of modern social life, an assumed bedrock upon which we base many of our decisions, yet this is a 'truly Promethean' development.[8] It poses huge difficulties for a religious tradition which throughout much of its history has been deeply suspicious of sexuality and regarded procreation as the main positive justification for (penetrative) sexual activity. Whilst many

Christians 'know' that pre-marital sex is wrong for them, they have forgotten the 'real' reason for this being the case, forgotten what lies at the heart of the prohibition. It is of course quite simple: the creation of a new human life is a weighty ethical matter, and it should only occur within a relationship that is capable of bringing that baby through to adulthood with the appropriate nurture and guidance. With the advent of highly effective contraception this traditional cornerstone to sexual ethics, often obscured by the elaborate edifice which has been placed upon it, has been removed. What we have witnessed then in the last thirty years is the edifice of Christian sexual ethics teetering over the gap in its foundations. For many prudent, morally serious young people, the absolute prohibition on pre-marital sexuality cannot be sustained purely because it is asserted by the Church. The Church has accepted in principle the permissibility of contraception, which constitutes a fundamental break within the Christian tradition, yet it has, I believe, consistently underestimated the consequences of that stance.

Furthermore, cohabitation has firmly eclipsed marriage as the marker for first partnerships between men and women. Whereas around one in twenty women marrying for the first time in the late 1960s had cohabited before the marriage ceremony, by the end of the 1990s that proportion had risen to nearly eight in ten, and I have very little doubt that it has continued to rise. This has transformed a radical, or at least unconventional, lifestyle decision courting social disapproval into something not remarked upon even in the children of Anglican bishops and Tory MPs. Cohabitation is now the main route into marriage. Furthermore, the majority of the adults in most western countries hold the belief that it is prudent to cohabit before marriage, that it is the right, the moral course of action, and by implication that to countenance undergoing a marriage ceremony before living together might be considered an irresponsible course of action.

Such apparent discontinuity with the past poses a challenge to Christian thinking and practice especially for an established church whose vocation is to serve the wider community, not least through the pastoral offices. Yet whilst there has been pastoral adjustment to the reality of cohabitation, there has been little sustained theological exploration of the subject. The Church teaches, and is perceived to teach, that marriage begins with a ceremony in a church (usually on a Saturday afternoon in the summer), and that sexual intercourse or cohabitation before that point constitutes a transgression.

Becoming married

In this book I intend a reappraisal of this state of affairs. At the heart of its argument, is a call for a renewed understanding that becoming married is a process that may take place over months or perhaps years, and that cohabitation can come to be seen as a natural part of this process. In this I am being highly unoriginal, for the idea that a marriage might begin with a religious ceremony, rather than that ceremony solemnising a marriage, is a rather recent idea in Christian thinking. For, whilst the Western Church had always sought to control and regulate marriage practices, where it has been able to do so, it was not until the Council of Trent in 1563 that the Roman Catholic Church's liturgical involvement was seen as essential to the validity of a marriage. In Protestant Britain it was the introduction of the public registration of marriage with the Hardwicke Act of 1753 that marked the watershed establishing in its long wake the ceremonial 'theory' of marriage as a social 'fact'. Prior to this legislation, which extended the power of the State over the individual and was regarded in its day by many as a gross infringement upon personal liberty by an interfering State, a range of informal marriage practices was widespread. The most important of these was betrothal.

Betrothal, in early modern England, involved the expression of intent to marry usually accompanied by the exchange of tokens between the couple, with cohabitation and a sexual relationship habitually following this commitment. The understanding being that, unless pregnancy ensued, which obliged the man to marry, the betrothal could be broken by either party. Such a phase of provisional commitment was entered upon with the clear expectation that marriage was the desired, but not the inevitable, outcome.

Given that perhaps the most distinctive feature of Christianity's teaching on marriage (*vis-a-vis* the other major religious traditions) has been its 'tough' line on divorce, or to put it another way, its insistence on 'lifelong marriage as the unchanging ideal', a more gradual induction into the 'institution' of marriage makes a good deal of sense, especially, it might be argued in a high-divorce culture. And indeed a number of Christian writers including Canon Anthony Harvey, Bishop Kenneth Stevenson, Professor Adrian Thatcher and the prominent Roman Catholic psychiatrist Jack Dominian have, from a variety of perspectives, advocated some sort of 'revival' of this practice of betrothal.[9] As an expression of the desire to reconnect church life with the everyday domestic environment and to engage with the social and psychological realities that becoming married involves, this proposal has much to commend it. However, as Helen Oppenheimer has pointed out – there is an obvious problem with this.[10]

One of the central convictions of this book, and one that is often forgotten in the debate about cohabitation and marriage, is that marriage practices cannot be separated from their social context. Marriage is an economic, legal, psychological, social and even political reality. It has taken quite different forms at different periods in history as a result of the interaction of demographic regimes, mentalité and economic structure, to delineate three central dimensions that profoundly affect its shape and content. So, to give one small example, much of the wise compassionate language in the Anglican teaching document, *Marriage*, assumes an equality of men and women unimaginable before the last century, an equality based *de facto* upon the fact that women have been liberated from the relentless cycle of pregnancy, childbirth and child-rearing. Furthermore, the tone of this document owes at least as great a debt to twentieth-century reflection on the insights of psychology as to historic Christian thinking about marriage.

Quite simply, many aspects of marriage which we assume to be fundamental were not so for the vast majority of Christians through history. Prior to the eighteenth century, there is, for example, much less concern about whether a couple loved each other, indeed given the life expectancy of the time, such emotional dependence might well have been regarded as foolishness. Instead, stress was laid upon the fulfilment of conjugal duties: the emphasis of marriage was upon its economic advantages and the production and rearing of legitimate children. As a corollary, the choice of a partner was primarily the task of parents, other kin and friends.

In the last 150 years three closely related developments have been hugely important in shaping and reshaping marriage: the decline in infant and child mortality and the increase in adult life expectancy; the emancipation of women; and, I would argue most importantly of all, especially in relation to the development of cohabitation, the widespread acceptance of contraceptives and the moral endorsement by the churches of their use (with one notable exception). It is in light of these changes that contemporary cohabitation must be understood and evaluated.

'Reading' cohabitation

The churches have tended to 'read' contemporary cohabitation as a rejection of marriage and a clear example of the waning influence of its teaching. Some of the more generous discussions have considered cohabitation to be a 'mixed bag', dividing cohabiting relationships into three camps based upon perceived motivations: the casual, the ideological and the committed. Those in the first category are not interested in the permanent commitment of marriage and are in their relationship for its immediate benefits only; those in the second consciously 'reject' the institution of marriage for a number of reasons; whilst those in the third group see cohabitation in some sense as preparatory for marriage, are committed to and envisage a future together, and having taken several steps along the way, might be deemed in most senses 'already married'. Naturally it is this third category that is viewed most positively by the Church.

There are, I would like to argue, serious difficulties with this rather neat typology: it conveys no sense of the relative importance of the various dispositions; it presents an over-rational, simplified and static conception of people's intentions; and it tends to lead to a lack of engagement with the practices and ideas associated with the first two categories. Most fundamentally of all, it isolates and perceives cohabitation as a problematic phenomenon completely separate from that of marriage. This is a quite bizarre 'ring-fencing' activity in a society in which four in ten marriages, a great many solemnised in a Christian ceremony, end in divorce.

We might go on to enquire, for example, what those who 'reject' marriage are actually turning their back on? For some, it may be a conscious rejection of what lies at the heart of marriage, namely the possibility of a permanent, sexually exclusive relationship: such people may quite consciously be engaged in a life in which one 'temporary meaningless relationship' devoid of significant commitment is replaced by another. For most people, however, I would suggest, it is not the aspiration for a permanent and sexually exclusive relationship that is being consciously denied (even if people are pessimistic about its realisation), rather it is the cultural 'clothing' of marriage that is being rejected. In particular, it is the 'institutional' dimension, the public and legal aspects of marriage which are often objected to in favour of an emphasis upon the private significance ascribed to the relationship by the couple. Such a rejection is part and parcel of a much wider rejection of the institutional elements of society and constitutes part of the ongoing three-way tussle between State, Church and individuals over the 'ownership' of marriage. Here, those Christians who denounce cohabitation because it lacks a public dimension need to be cautious. What is pertinent about this criticism, from the perspective of the Christian tradition, is not the involvement of the state *per se*, but the public recognition of the status of the relationship by the community which is significant to the couple in question. That *could* take place in a church on a summer's afternoon, but it *might* occur at a housewarming party with the commitment that a joint mortgage brings, just as, prior to 1753, the intention to 'live together as man and wife' was often expressed and witnessed in a range of social locations including the English public house.[11]

Another reason that 'marriage' might be rejected is because of its historical associations with male authority and the sense that being married brings traditional roles for women and men, that the individuals concerned may wish to reject. Again such a rejection, which is equally an assertion of values of mutuality and equality, is not novel. Examples of women using unofficial forms of marriage to mitigate the discriminating aspects of formal marriage can be found in many societies from first-century Rome to the nineteenth-century Lancashire cotton mills.

The importance of stability

This book is concerned with how marriages come into being and whether cohabitation has a legitimate role in that process. Yet this is not, in my opinion, the most important or pressing ethical issue relating to marriage. That status should be reserved for the issue of marital breakdown and divorce. On this, it is worth quoting Jack Dominian who has some characteristically strong words on the subject:

> It seems to me that, as far as Christianity is concerned, the changes in marriage and marital breakdown have to become an urgent priority, eclipsing all other social issues . . . marriage and the family are the root of society and the Church, and when they are in distress everything suffers in consequence. All we do is spend money and resources to look after disturbed children in schools and clinics, sick people in surgeries, delinquents in court, build more abodes to house the divorced couple, spend billions to ward off economic distress and, above all, create a vicious circle in which the divorced children of today are the divorced parents of tomorrow. It is astonishing how little importance has been paid by church leaders, with few exceptions, to this issue. The silence has been incomprehensible.[12]

The implications of cohabitation for the subsequent stability of marriages should then rightly form part of the Christian evaluation of living together, and it is perhaps for this reason that the Anglican bishops regarded pre-marital cohabitation as 'exposed to uncertainties and tensions' and therefore 'not to be recommended'. This would be a natural conclusion if the bishops had appropriated the research of social scientists into cohabitation in the 1980s. To the genuine surprise of many researchers and journalists, by 1990 a number of studies clearly showed that those who cohabited before marriage were more, rather than less, likely to divorce after they had married.[13] The simplest, most popular, but incorrect, interpretation of this finding was that the experience of pre-marital cohabitation had a destabilising effect on subsequent marriage. Were this true, couples would be much better to heed the bishops' advice and marry directly rather than live together first. Subsequently it has become clear, however, that this statistical finding is in fact far better explained by a 'compositional effect'. That is, that those who cohabited initially were social 'innovators', unconventional or progressive individuals quite prepared to risk condemnation by conventional society; such individuals tended to be disproportionately irreligious and included a good number of people rejecting marriage for ideological reasons. It is unsurprising that as a group they were less likely to feel bound by the idea that marriage was for life when many of them did decide to marry. More recent research, conducted when a majority of those marrying have cohabited first, has shown that it is no longer the case that those who cohabit in preparation for marriage are more likely to get divorced after the event.[14] Furthermore, most cohabitations remain short-lived, ending in separation or in marriage within three years.

Cohabitation: a 'trailer' for marriage?

Along with other evidence,[15] this suggests that the majority of young people seek a marriage, as it has been traditionally understood by the Christian Church: an exclusive, permanent relationship within which they might have children. However, they regard it as prudent to live together first, not, as has been suggested by some, as a way of putting marriage 'on trial' as if conducting a human experiment, but rather as a 'trailer' for the absolute commitment that marriage entails. For many (I grant not all), cohabitation is not only a period of provisional commitment, but also of movement towards the asking of a question which expects the answer 'yes'. For a generation born into a mass divorce culture, there is a morally informed caution within the experience of contemporary cohabitation, which takes seriously the warning, that none should enter upon the commitment of marriage 'lightly or selfishly'. At a time when marriage is widely seen as problematic, such caution merits intelligent engagement and encouragement from the churches, rather than a wagging finger.

Yet rather than enter upon the nitty-gritty issues of teaching people how to build intimacy and trust, how to communicate and negotiate difference, or even commend the centrality of Christian forgiveness as essential to a relationship which can be life-enhancing, many Christians often remain obsessed with issues of sexuality. It would, of course, be absurd to deny the centrality of sexuality to human living, yet the way in which this is expressed by the churches suggests that the regulation of sexuality has a powerful symbolic function, drawing boundaries in ways that are increasing incomprehensible to those outside the Church. The bishops' teaching document on marriage speaks of our society, with some cause, as fostering 'all kinds of misleading fantasies about sex'. However, in considering whether sexual intercourse might be permissible in a faithful, exclusive relationship upstream of the 'I do' of ceremonial commitment, the Christian tradition itself might need some probing for its own 'misleading fantasies'. Let us then first turn to the question of sex and what it might be for.

CHAPTER TWO

Not in the passion of lust

At the heart of, or as often underlying, much Christian discussion about contemporary cohabitation, lies anxiety about what sex is for. Although today most churches view sexual desire as a natural and right constituent of a love between a man and a woman[1] involving the heart and mind as well as the body, such an understanding is comparatively recent, and runs counter to the weight of Christian tradition. For historically, Christianity has overwhelmingly taken a much more pessimistic approach regarding procreation as the only positive justification for sexual activity and the avoidance of fornication a good reason for marriage. This pessimistic evaluation can be clearly illustrated from the preface to the marriage service used for over 400 years in England and Wales on the 'happy day' which warns that the estate of Holy Matrimony should not be entered into 'to satisfy men's carnal lusts and appetites, like brute beasts that have no understanding.'[2] The deep suspicion that sex is inherently sinful has not disappeared, rather it forms part of our inherited cultural baggage – it often lies just below the surface. Indeed the oft quoted remark attributed to Saint Jerome that a man who loved his wife too ardently was an adulterer, was echoed as recently as October 1980, when, during the synod on the Family, Pope John Paul II declared at a weekly audience that a married man was morally guilty of adultery if he looked at his own wife with sexual desire.[3]

So, have modern Christians got it wrong? Is an account of

sexuality which in broad terms regards it as a necessary evil redeemed in part by procreation, an integral part of the Gospel message? If not, what account of sexuality should Christians seek to give in a society in which sexuality has effectively become separated from procreation through the widespread acceptance of contraception? What is sex for and what are the limits of its expression?

In this chapter we will explore these questions through a consideration of two competing voices which exist within the tradition. The historically dominant voice has seen sex as an evil necessary for the survival of the race; the 'lesser voice' has taken a more positive stance and regarded sexuality as an important dimension of the love between a man and a woman. I will argue that the first of these voices has been unduly affected by the influence of Roman and particularly Stoic[4] ways of thinking about the body, whilst the latter may resonate more accurately with the biblical account.

The necessary evil

Historians and philosophers have argued that the cultural attitudes to sexuality and the body, which can be described as characteristic of western civilisation, were forged in the crucible of Christian late antiquity, that is in the third and fourth centuries AD. Not only did Christians possess a distinctive approach to such matters, but also it seems, this had become a touchstone of Christian identity fundamental to distinguishing it from its pagan surroundings. With the triumph of the Emperor Constantine and the subsequent Christianisation of the Empire, this new *mentalité* took root and has dominated western thinking down to our own times, most especially within Roman Catholicism. A defining aspect of this mentalité was the idea that sexual intercourse had only one truly legitimate end, namely procreation.

The first Christians

The first Christians inherited and worked from Jewish assumptions about sexuality. In Judaism, the fundamental approach to sexuality could be described as one of unsentimental realism. The inevitability of sexual expression and a recognition of the role of pleasure was combined with an acute awareness of the inherent dangers – sexuality needed to be channelled and controlled. Human sexual love was, for example, clearly celebrated as something inherently good in the Song of Songs, and could even function allegorically for the expression of divine love. As a corollary to this, and in opposition to the fertility cults of the Ancient Near East, adultery, fornication and other forms of sexual licence including homosexuality were seen as forms of apostasy profaning the holiness of God.

The sexual morality that the early Christians inherited from this Jewish background was thus one which was stricter than that of its neighbours and concerned with maintaining clear boundaries between the holy and the impure: the people of God and unbelievers. So, for example in his first letter to the Thessalonians, probably the oldest extant Christian writing (AD 50), St Paul reminds his fellow Christian brothers that among other things, they should take a wife 'in holiness and honour not in the passion of lust like heathen that do not know God' (1 Thess. 4:4–5). This passage is one of a number in which the apostle seeks to distinguish between Christians and outsiders on the basis of their sexual restraint and marital discipline. And well he might make such a distinction, for the Greco-Roman world within which the Christians sought to live 'unto the Lord' was one in which the range and variety of acceptable sexual practices was extensive.

Roman sexual mores at the time of Jesus' birth were dominated by the dictates of social status, in particular by the well-established notion that men should avoid effeminacy and the shame of passionate or emotional dependence on inferiors. Traditionally, conjugal love between husband and wife was considered to be both ridiculous and impossible, and a free man was at liberty to engage in sexual acts with slaves, prostitutes and concubines without incurring the penalties attached to adultery, defined as intercourse with a married woman – an offence against her husband. Furthermore, homosexual and heterosexual love were not in general morally differentiated by Roman commentators; indeed the 'Greek love' between men was to a degree idealised (in a similar fashion to 'romantic love' in western culture) but strictly on the proviso that the upper-class male was in no way 'infected' by the experience through taking the passive role or through emotional dependence on his partner. Sexual actions were thus not problematic so long as they were exactly that – actions – undertaken in a hierarchical context, against (as it were) others. Maintaining clear social distance between the sexual agent and those with whom he chose to have sex left the male citizen untainted. Boys were socialised into this world at puberty, an occurrence virtually synonymous with sexual initiation with a prostitute, slave or concubine with the decade between puberty and marriage not infrequently regarded as a time for socially sanctioned sexual licence.

The fear of shame flowing from attachment to or subordination to an inferior was intimately connected with, or perhaps underwritten by, physiological beliefs which resulted in a wariness of excessive sexual pleasuring. Although sexual activity was thought by many in the ancient world to be good for the health, the belief that the release of semen was an enfeebling action was also widespread and a number of prominent writers presented the sexual act as dangerous and harmful to health.[5] Women, by contrast, were not thought to be so affected by the sexual act and, although the virginity of women at marriage was sacrosanct and marital fidelity was sought and praised in married women, infidelity was not a matter of great public consequence. Divorce, at the desire of either partner was easy, common and carried no stigma. Roman citizens were, it has been asserted, puritans – of a sort – unconcerned with conjugality and reproduction, but obsessed with virility and the threats to it.[6]

'Eunuchs for the Kingdom'

Between the death of the apostle Paul and the triumph of Christianity with Constantine in AD 312, a deeply ascetic tradition evolved which placed a great value on virginity and made a correspondingly poor evaluation of the married state. Not only was celibacy highly valued, it was even advocated within marriage where it came to be understood that sexual intercourse was legitimated by the need for procreation alone. This appears to have been a radical innovation quite at odds with both what is known of the Jewish tradition either before or after Jesus and with the 'the passions of the Gentiles'. Where then did such a notion come from?

One possibility is that this ascetic thread within Christianity had its origins with the Jesus movement itself: that Christianity was born of a radical variant of Judaism inherently ambivalent to the body and sexuality. There certainly existed a number of communities made up of celibates in Palestine at the time of Jesus, something known to us from the writings of Pliny, Philo, Josephus and from the Dead Sea Scrolls. In addition, within the gospels there are highly ambivalent statements concerning marriage and family life. Within Luke's gospel, for example, Jesus asserts that:

> The sons of this age marry and are given in marriage; but those who are accounted worthy to attain to that age and to the resurrection of the dead neither marry nor are they given in marriage, for they cannot die any more because

they are equal to angels and are sons of God, being sons of the resurrection. (Luke 20:34–36)

Or again, there is the teaching which 'not all can receive' concerning the 'eunuchs for the sake of the kingdom of God' (Matthew 19:11–12).

There is, however, a more plausible origin for this development. The second-century convert from paganism, Justin (martyred around AD 165), spoke for many when he wrote that 'whatever all have said well belongs to us Christians'. With the diffusion of Christianity and the distancing from its Jewish roots, it was increasingly to Greek and Roman philosophy and particularly to the later Stoics that many turned to appropriate what had been 'said well'. Such Stoic philosophers exhorted their elite audience of upper-class men to live according to the universal law of the cosmos, to rise above the passions and through the use of will to be dutiful and model citizens. For them marriage was intimately connected with citizenship (large numbers of people in the Roman Empire were excluded from legal marriage on account of their status as non-citizens), and constituted a political and civic duty, as important to the maintenance of the city as the fortification of its walls. Although citations of the philosophers are legion in the works of the early Christian intellectuals, one who seems to have been particularly important in his influence over Christians' attitudes to marriage and sexuality was the distinguished knight (of Etruscan origin), Musonius Rufus (born c. AD 30). Musonius appears to have held some extreme views by contemporary standards; in particular he expresses a distinct distaste for pleasure, which he argues is a sign of decadence. Indeed, he is recorded as arguing that 'the pursuit of mere pleasure, even in marriage is unjust and against the law.' Rather, procreation alone can justify sexual intercourse. Unsurprisingly, then, he argues that a man of self-control 'would not dare to approach a

prostitute, a free woman outside marriage, or even by God
his own female slave.'[7] The inclusion of this last category
constituted a radical challenge to the cultural assumptions of
his contemporaries, for whom there was no discernible wrong
in such sexual encounters, for 'no one' (i.e. no citizen) would
be harmed, quite unlike the case of adultery, in which a man
would harm the husband of a married woman with whom he
had a liaison. Musonius, however, argues that even sex with
a slave is shameful, not because it is an abuse of power which
dehumanises the slave, but because it lessens the man in
question, for he is 'mastered' by his passions.[8]

Musonius' influence on his contemporaries was, for all we
know, negligible, but perhaps because he also condemned
other 'Gentile lusts', homosexuality and adultery, as *tolmena
para phusin* ('an outrage against nature') early Christians
recognised a kindred spirit. The philosopher convert, Justin,
follows him in arguing that the only reasonable, natural, and
therefore right, use of sexuality was for procreation and states
for the first time within the tradition that Christians understand this principle and indeed follow it, claiming that
Christians only ever engage in sex for the procreation of
children. This idea begins to take root in the Christian households of the second and third centuries and finds its warmest
expression in the writings of Clement of Alexandria (c.
150–215). Clement draws heavily on the writings of Musonius
and fellow Stoics and weaves them together with Christian
sources to present what is in many ways an exalted vision of
conjugal love, yet one in which the monogamous Christian
couple engage in sexual intercourse solely to the end of procreation. Such a stance forms part of a broad apologetic thrust
aimed at claiming the moral high ground, demonstrating not
just the compatibility of Christianity with the very best of
Greco-Roman culture but also the practical fulfilment of such
philosophical ideals in the Christian faith. In the strange new
clothes of Christian asceticism, the Stoic ideal, advocated for

voluntary adoption by the few, found itself central to the teaching of an increasingly popular and widespread religion. As the historian, Peter Brown, notes:

> What the ancient philosophers presented as further refinement, tentatively added to an ancient and inward-looking morality of the elite, became in the hands of Christian teachers, the foundation for the construction of a whole new building that embraced all classes in its demands.[9]

The Stoic injunction to train the instincts in the pursuit of rational goals alone was thus written into the lives of Christians. The ideal was not to experience at all.[10] Virginity and lifelong celibacy were widely promoted and practised and even the world of the subconscious was colonised: sexual dreams and nocturnal emissions, or rather the lack of them, were regarded as crucial indicators on the journey into holiness by the burgeoning ranks of monks. The body, its sexuality and the status of marriage became highly contested subjects in an intense theological and cultural battleground.

For some bishops and theologians like Saint Jerome, deeply enamoured of the virtue of virginity, a fully committed Christian life was barely possible for the married person who indulged the sexual instinct – even for procreative ends. Others, including the most influential writer on the subject, Saint Augustine (to whom we shall return in Chapter 4), took a more moderate view. In his work, *On the Good of Marriage*, he outlined three benefits or 'goods' of the union: the most concrete of these goods was unsurprisingly children; the second faithfulness, though this was primarily conceived in the negative – as a way of avoiding the evils of fornication; and finally, sacrament, a more positive affirmation that marriage symbolised the union of Christ with his Church.

Whilst Augustine's writings were more moderate than many of his contemporaries, and carved out a space for the married person within the Christian community against those who would see them almost completely marginalized, his theological elaboration of the nature and meaning of sexual intercourse left a highly ambivalent inheritance, for, according to the African bishop, sexual intercourse was inevitably sinful, as it was through the sexual act that original sin was transmitted from Adam and Eve relentlessly from generation to generation. Whilst God permitted sexual intercourse, forgiving it for the sake of producing children, it remained inherently sinful in itself and in its consequences, irrespective of the good intentions or piety of the participants. However hard the dutiful Christian tried to lie back and fix their mind on higher things – they were still embraced by (or embedded in) a state of sin.

Voices from the margins

Naturally there was dissent. Indeed, there were those who championed a different vision for the married in which sexual pleasure could be seen as morally neutral. One such, Julian, the married Bishop of Eclanum in Southern Italy, argued that sexuality was a neutral energy, a 'sixth sense' of the body. Nevertheless, such voices remained, like Julian himself, exiled on the margins of the tradition[11] by the application of a philosophical approach which rationalised and rationed sexuality to one positive function only – procreation.

Saint Augustine was bitterly opposed to his married episcopal colleague and scathing of the appeal to personal experience in his writings about the sexual instinct:

> Really, really: is that your experience? So you would not have married couples restrain that evil – I refer of course to your favourite good? So you would have them jump into bed whenever they like, whenever they feel tickled by desire. Far be it from them to postpone this itch til

bedtime: let's have your 'legitimate union of bodies' whenever your 'natural good' is excited. If this is the sort of married life you led, don't drag up your experience in debate . . .[12]

Augustine's pessimistic view of sexual intercourse as inherently sinful (though excused for the purpose of procreation and grudgingly permitted to prevent the greater evil of fornication or adultery) triumphed and remained the dominant theological understanding throughout the medieval period and beyond. Marriage is, however, too central to the workings of society for its meaning to be entirely prescribed by celibate churchmen. So, this theological inheritance was modulated somewhat by other influences on the practice and understanding of marriage – not least the law – for unlike theologians, legislators have to be firmly rooted in those issues generated by the 'lived-in' cultural reality of marriage, hence the enshrining of the 'conjugal debt' as a principle in canon law. Early medieval canonists of the twelfth century, like Gratian, Peter Lombard and others also tended to place greater emphasis on mutual affection between the sexes contributing to a gradual 'softening' of the earlier sexual asceticism.

A further important challenge to the dual inheritance of sexual pessimism and an austere patriarchy came in the twelfth century with the infusion of Christian culture by the ideal of courtly love – a chaste but adulatory form of idealised love which sprung from poetic forms developed in Provençal and was disseminated by groups of troubadours wandering from castle to castle. This emergence of romantic lyric poetry, in which a lower status man expresses a yearning, mysterious love for an unattainable upper-class woman raised the possibility of women possessing a greater autonomy, not just to attract but also to choose and reject. It is to this curious and obscure poetic source that the broad, winding river of romantic love which dominates the cultural landscape of today owes its origins.

It was the crisis in Christendom of the early sixteenth century that sowed the seeds for a positive re-evaluation of the relationship between sexuality and personhood which intimately linked sexual intercourse to the experiencing of legitimate pleasure as a constituent part of marital affection. For with the Reformation came clerical marriage and theologians could once again speak with the authority of experience. As a result, a deeper appreciation of the role of companionship in marriage emerged. Whilst patristic writers wrote highly of mutual affection between husband and wife and a number of medieval (celibate) theologians, most notably Aquinas placed a greater emphasis on the role of friendship within marriage, the Reformation brought a number of men who knew something of marriage. One such was Thomas Cranmer's domestic chaplain Thomas Becon (1511–1567) who in his popular writings favourably contrasted marriage with celibates, who were, in his eyes; ' . . . monsters of nature for their sterility and barrenness [who] die as unprofitable clods of earth'[13] and condemned men who didn't listen to their wives, for as he pointed out, women often gave better advice than men. Another was the leading continental Reformer, Martin Bucer (1491–1551), a close friend of the Archbishop, who argued that the three reasons Christians gave for marriage (first procreation, then the avoidance of fornication and finally mutual companionship) should be radically re-ordered:

> Now the proper end of marriage is not copulation or children . . . but the full and proper and main end of marriage, is the communicating of all duties, both human and divine, each to other with utmost benevolence and affection.[14]

Bucer's view, shared by a number of influential theologians

including Erasmus, that social companionship lay at the very heart of marriage had a profound influence upon Archbishop Thomas Cranmer (along with his sixteen-year marriage to Margaret) as he set about constructing a new marriage service for a newly Protestant nation. Whilst that new marriage service looks much like its Catholic predecessor, and *contra* Bucer places 'mutuall societie, helpe and comfort' third in a list of reasons for marriage – it is with this, the 1549 Prayer Book, that mutual companionship is named in public liturgy for the first time as a reason for matrimony.[15] It is also Cranmer who introduces at the culmination of the vows; the promise 'to love and to cherish'.

From this foundation of companionship, the idea that delight or pleasure taken in the act of sexual intercourse might form a natural and legitimate part of marital affection begins to emerge in the writings of several seventeenth-century Anglicans (and others, e.g. Milton) including John Donne and most explicitly with Bishop Jeremy Taylor (1613–1667) – another bishop dragging his personal experience into the debate!

> ... although in this [act], as in eating and drinking, there is an appetite to be satisfied, which cannot be done without pleasing that desire; yet since that desire and satisfaction was intended by Nature for other ends, they should never be seperated from those ends, but always be joyned with all or one of these ends; *with a desire of children, or to avoyd fornication, or to lighten and ease the cares and sadnesses of houshold affairs, or to endear each other*; but never with a purpose either in act or desire, to separate the sensuality from those ends which hallow it.[16]

Taylor's warm words come in the context of giving spiritual guidance to married couples rather than in a more explicitly theological work or indeed as one speaking on behalf of the

Church. Consistent with this advice, Taylor also denounced the custom of enforced abstinence from sexual intercourse on the wedding night, before receiving communion and during Lent.[17] Rather, the case for sexual intercourse as an expression of personal love and a source of emotional bonding between wife and husband had to wait until the twentieth century before it found more widespread support in the official statements of the churches. Perhaps one of its clearest expressions is to found in an Anglican report of 1978, *Marriage and the Church's Task*, which speaks of a 'polyphony of love' that:

> ... finds expression in the lovers' bodily union. This is not to be comprehended simply in terms of two individuals' experience of ecstatic pleasure. Such it certainly may be, but it is always more. It is an act of personal commitment that spans past, present and future. It is a celebration, healing, renewed pledge and promise. Sexual intercourse can 'mean' many different things to husband and wife, according to mood and circumstance. Above all, it communicates the affirmation of mutual belonging.[18]

Such an understanding of sexual expression within marriage is startling when, give or take the odd married bishop, it is contrasted with the weight of the Christian witness. Does it, and similar statements from other denominations, represent a legitimate development of Christian, particularly Protestant, experience and understanding or is it an accommodation to the spirit of the age, to the insights of twentieth-century psychology? Has the influence of Freud or Kinsey been more telling in such matters than that of Saint Augustine?

Despite the dominance of the anti-sexual emphasis from the second century onwards, this 'new' understanding of sexuality does find resonance with a small handful of brave 'soloists', who have cried out in the barren and silent wilderness of a largely ascetic tradition. Yet at the heart of Christian self-understanding, our primary documents, the scriptures, approach marriage through the language and symbolism of the 'one flesh', an idea which suggests that not only is sexual expression integral to personal love, but that the sexual union can in fact be regarded as, in some sense, constitutive of the marriage union (as several medieval canonists sought to establish). Indeed, it might seem extraordinary given the centrality that the idea of the 'one flesh' has within the biblical account, that the Christian faith, with its additional emphasis on the incarnation, has been held captive to a negative view of the place of sexual intercourse in the man–woman relationship. It is worth considering, then, the possibility that beyond these 'voices from the margin' there is a deeper resonance with the *basso profoundo* of scripture.

One flesh

The Jewish inheritance

Our starting point, naturally enough, is the book of Genesis. Here, there are two accounts given for the creation of the human. The second and better known account (Gen. 2:18–25), (which is also likely to be the older account) starts with the 'lonely man' who has a rib removed from him in his sleep to generate his companion. This is probably intended to be an aetiological or 'just so' story explaining the strength of attraction that naturally exists between the sexes: because they were once one 'bone of my bones, flesh of my flesh' (Gen. 2:23), there is then a strong drive to be reunited.

> Therefore a man leaves his father and his mother and cleaves to his wife and they become one flesh. (Gen. 2:24)

This is not a statement which makes reference to custom or legal practice amongst the early Israelites (on the contrary, evidence suggests that women left their families to be integrated into their husband's family), rather it is concerned to convey the fact that the desire to pair is part of the divine ordering of creation. Thus coming together is not primarily for procreation, but for companionship, for the enhancement of interpersonal love. The oldest, foundational account of the purpose of sexual intercourse focuses therefore upon the relational rather than the procreative aspect of the sexual act.

Clearly sexual consummation lies to the fore in the idea of the 'one flesh', and in consummation of their love, the couple in some sense restore the original pattern of human unity. Such unity has extensive resonance throughout the scriptures, as Derrick Bailey in his ground-breaking book *The Mystery of Love and Marriage* put it:

> The singleness for which 'one' stands, in its most pregnant use, is organic, not arithmetical, and has a suggestion of uniqueness; it is exemplified at its highest in the mysterious triunity of the one God, of which the biunity of husband and wife is an analogue ... It is a union of the entire man and the entire woman. In it they become a new and distinct unity, wholly differing from and set over against other human relational unities, such as the family or the race.[19]

Indeed, the metaphor of love between husband and wife in marriage becomes a powerful and central one in the articulation of Jewish monotheism from the period of the exile in Babylon (597–538 BC) onwards (especially Hosea, but also Jeremiah, Ezekiel, Isaiah). It is a metaphor which finds new life evolving in the New Testament into the imagery of Christ and his bride the Church.

It is perhaps unsurprising, then, that there developed within Judaism a strong sense that an unmarried man was not a 'whole man' and that only upon the creation of the 'one person' in marriage could the image of God be discerned within them. This emphasis remains close to the heart of Jewish practice today:

> Marriage is not only the optimal way to live, but it is also central to the theology of Judaism. The entire success of the covenant rests on the marriage premise and its procreative impulse. The biological family, born of marriage, is the unit that carries the promises and the covenant, one generation at a time, toward their full completion and realisation.[20]

Whilst the primary reference is, of course, to the physical union established by sexual intercourse, as Bailey suggests, the union of the 'one flesh' involves the whole being and the personality at the deepest level. This holistic conception uniting personal identity and sexuality is in complete contradiction to Augustinian thinking. Indeed, in bringing the poison of erotic passion close to the chaste heart of faith the African bishop would regard such an understanding as morally corrosive. In this regard, if in no other, the intellectual giant of western Christendom is, I suggest, in error.

Nevertheless, the union of man and woman in 'one flesh' finds passionate scriptural expression in the unabashed eroticism of the Songs of Songs. This wonderful poem overflows with the language of yearning and desire. For here we read that she has ravished his heart ' . . . with a glance of [her] eyes' bringing forth from his lips a description of her delightfulness: her 'rounded thighs are like jewels', her 'navel a rounded bowl', her 'two breasts are like two fawns' and her 'kisses like the best wine that goes down smoothly gliding over lips and teeth' (S. of S. 4:9, 7:1–3, 9).

Not to be outdone, he is to her 'a bag of myrrh that lies between my breasts', whose 'eyes are like doves beside springs of water, bathed in milk', his 'body is ivory work, encrusted with sapphires' and his legs 'alabaster columns set upon bases of gold' (S. of S. 1:13, 5:12, 14–15).

Hardly surprising then, that she exclaims: 'O that his left hand were under my head, and that his right hand embraced me' (S. of S. 8:3).

Such unabashed eroticism is, of course, absent in the New Testament. However, the Hebraic idea of the 'one flesh' underpins the thought of both Jesus and Paul as they engage in vigorous debate with their opponents. For Jesus, the debate is with the Pharisees over the criteria for divorcing a wife. For Paul, it must be discerned from a heated dispute with the church in Corinth about the appropriateness of celibacy.

Jesus: 'no longer two'

Jewish approaches to divorce were framed by varying interpretations of Deuteronomy 24:1:

> When a man takes a wife and marries her, if then she finds no favour in his eyes because he has found some indecency in her, and he writes her a bill of divorce . . .

Divorce is clearly permitted by the text. The debate then revolves around what constitutes 'some indecency'. One school of interpretation associated with Rabbi Hillel took an indulgent view and regarded letting the food burn as indecent, the other associated with Rabbi Shammai, restricted the label to such matters as sexual misdemeanour.

In response then to the question posed by the Pharisees enquiring whether it was lawful for a man to divorce his wife, Jesus replies:

> Have you not read that he who made them from the beginning made them male and female, and said, 'For this reason a man shall leave his father and mother and be joined to his wife, and the two shall become one?' So they are no longer two but one. What God therefore has joined together, let no man put asunder. (Matt. 19:4b–6)

Jesus not only cites, and thereby lends authority to the two creation stories in the opening chapters of the book of Genesis (Gen. 1:26–30; 2:18–25), he also underlines and deepens the idea of the man–woman relationship as 'one flesh'. They are 'no longer two', but 'one flesh', a new entity of a deep personal union. Indeed the union is created by God himself and, as such, it is a permanent relationship. Here Jesus 'relocates' the institution of marriage from the domain of the Jewish law which treated the wife as the property of the husband back into the sphere of God's will. In so doing, Jesus provides a radical challenge to male autonomy which is consistent with his ministry and affirms the need for self-discipline and absolute commitment within marriage.

But it is to the apostle Paul we must turn for a more extensive consideration of the implications of the 'one flesh'.

Paul: against the celibates

In the seventh chapter of his letter to the Corinthians, of which the following verses are the most pertinent, Paul writes:

> [1]Now concerning the matters about which you wrote: 'It is well for a man not to touch a woman.'[2] But because of the temptation to immorality, each man should have his own wife and each woman her own husband.[3] The husband should give to his wife her conjugal rights, and likewise the wife to her husband.[4] For the wife does not rule her own body, but the husband does; likewise the husband does not rule over his own body, but the wife does.[5] Do not refuse one another except perhaps by agreement for a season, that you may devote yourselves to prayer; but then come together again, lest Satan tempt you through lack of self-control. I say this by way of concession, not of command. (1 Cor. 7:1–6)

Traditionally, the opening statement – 'It is well for a man not to touch a woman' – has been interpreted within the

Christian tradition as expressing Paul's fundamental opinion on the matter, an understanding consistent with the traditionally negative view of sex within marriage: that, whilst it isn't morally bad to have sexual relations within marriage – it is a still better thing not to be so indulgent. Such an interpretation naturally leads to the conclusion that Paul's tone is predominantly one of condescension to marriage – its permissibility a reluctant concession on account of the pervasive draw of *porneia* in Corinth.

Modern scholarship, however, interprets this line as a Corinthian slogan that Paul is quoting back to the letter's recipients in Corinth, i.e. in his letter to the Corinthians Paul is addressing a group of Christians who were zealous advocates of celibacy both within marriage and without. Such zeal it seems was putting pressure on members of the Corinthian congregation to dissolve their marriages in favour of celibacy or to practise sexual abstinence within marriage. Such an advocacy was rooted in and consistent with a 'spiritualised eschatology' – that is a belief that they were already living the life of the 'resurrection of the dead': they were spiritualised beings who spoke in the tongues of angels (glossolalia) and shunned participation in mere earthly existence including the state of marriage which clearly would pass away.[21] They were, in short, heaven-bent on celibacy.

One of the main thrusts of the letter as a whole is Paul's desire to counter this 'spiritualised eschatology'. Rather than advocating an ascetic lifestyle *per se*, Paul's reasons for preferring the single state are purely pragmatic and flow from his dominating concern, the eschatological imperative. Believers are categorically not 'already there' in some spiritual sense, rather he and his fellow Christians are living in the last days. Paul's exhortations and judgements are therefore 'emergency measures': the time is short, to marry is to take upon oneself an unnecessary burden and distraction from the pressing reality that lies just around the corner of time, the *parousia*, the second coming of the Lord. In the light of this, I would suggest, Paul displays a compassionate, realistic and unabashed approach to sexuality within marriage. Indeed, in the face of such an imminent and pressing reality, the choice for celibacy is an entirely reasonable one. It does not reflect any negativity towards sexual expression within marriage.

In fact, a careful analysis shows that Paul regards abstinence within marriage as strictly forbidden except in the most exceptional of circumstances. The emphasis in verse 2 that 'each man should have his own wife' and vice versa lies not upon the 'each' underlining the importance of exclusive monogamy (polygamy was not an issue of the day), but upon the sexual nature of the 'have'.[22] In response to the 'unilateral' rejection of the marriage bed by some, Paul advocates full, mutual sexual relations as a due within marriage. The stress then is upon mutual responsibility and indebtedness, rather than duty, though it doesn't entirely exclude the latter. Indeed, the spirit of Paul's exposition would not be out of place in a contemporary marriage guidance manual.[23]

Paul's central point is that the married person does not have authority over his or her body to do with as (s)he might wish. Here Paul is keen to counter a Corinthian watchword, 'freedom'; the married are not free to use their bodies as they wish with no regard for their spouses – rather they have an obligation to their spouses. So in addition to precluding men from uniting their bodies with prostitutes, slave girls or concubines (see 1 Cor. 6:15–17), Paul is also insisting that women and men cannot deny their spouses sex on account of the 'higher' religious goal of prayer. In this his teaching is entirely consistent with the spirit of Rabbinic teaching both then and now, for within Judaism a newly married man is excused the obligation to say the Sh^{e}ma.[24]

The strength of Paul's commitment to the full mutuality of sexuality within marriage is made strikingly in verse 5: 'Do not refuse each other' is in fact better translated as 'stop defrauding' or 'stop robbing' one another (in this matter), with the clear implication that in so doing spouses are taking away something which rightfully belongs, not to them, but to the other. Similarly, the concession to abstinence is striking in its qualification, being (i) tentative ('unless perhaps'); (ii) grudging ('by mutual agreement'); and, (iii) temporary ('for a set time only'). It is also worth noting that sexual abstinence is to create the leisure for prayer – there is no implication here of the widespread idea that sexual intercourse is polluting and renders individuals incapable of prayer.

In direct contradiction to some of his subsequent Christian interpreters, Paul is opposed root and branch to abstinence within marriage. Indeed, in the final verse quoted he is swift to ensure that those advocating sexual abstinence get the message loud and clear. For this temporary, mutually agreed abstinence for the purpose of prayer is a concession to their desire for abstinence and emphatically not a command: 'I am not commanding that you take times of sexual abstinence for prayer' so the argument goes, 'merely pointing out that sexual abstinence is only acceptable when it meets these criteria'.[25]

Given the dominant patriarchal ethos of the surrounding culture enshrining male rights, the repeated emphasis upon the equal and reciprocal rights of the wife and husband is extraordinary. Indeed, Paul promotes one of the highest views of sexual relations within marriage to be found. Subsequent interpretation of the passage in terms of the 'conjugal debt' as a husband's privilege and a wife's obligation is a crass simplification of the mutuality within marriage that Paul advocates. Ownership and independence is what Paul is seeking to oppose, rather the emphasis is upon belonging: 'not on "you owe me" but on "I owe you" '.[26]

In short, Paul is sober and level-headed about marriage, his view of it has been characterised in the following terms: ' . . . marriage is at worse troublesome, is in no way wrong, and is a divine institution.'[27] It is the norm within the Christian community and a full partnership can be a place for the cultivation of holiness (1 Thess. 4:4 and 1 Cor. 7:15). As such this approach is clearly rooted in his Jewish inheritance and finds clear echoes in near contemporary rabbinical teaching.

In writing to the Corinthians, Paul seeks to draw a distinction between two alternative Christian paths, that of the celibate and that of the married householder, and there is no hint in his writings that the married person should aspire to the sexual abstinence of the celibate. His preference for the single state reflects neither a negative attitude to the material world, nor to the human body. Rather it is practical preference, a 'sign of the times' which are, in his expectation, coming swiftly to an end. For within the generation of his readers, he expects there to be those who will be alive, who will be ' . . . left until the coming of the Lord' (1 Thess. 4:15).

A generation or so later, when the intensity of expectation is more muted, it is perhaps unsurprising to find, at least in the Pastoral Epistles,[28] a quite different picture painted from that of Paul's Corinth. To be married has become a pre-requisite for church leadership as an *episkopos*: 'Now a bishop must be above reproach, the husband of one wife.' Here the Christian leader is exhorted, doubtless with apologetic intent, to be an exemplary Roman citizen who 'must manage his household well, keeping his children submissive and respectful in every way' (1 Tim. 3:2, 4). Christians were thus to be seen as good citizens and the association between wisdom, required for leadership, and being married is one very much in company with developing Jewish ideas of the Rabbinate, for whom marriage became the near-compulsory criterion of the wise in the third and fourth centuries AD. Yet as we have outlined above, by this later period, ironically, the Corinthian slogan, 'It is good for a man not to touch a woman' had become the mission statement for a culture shaped by the aspiration to chastity – all but compulsory for the Christian leader and a perverse aspiration for many a Christian couple.

Christians had found, through their newly acquired attitude to sexuality, a way of demonstrating a righteousness greater than either the Gentiles or the spiritual descendants of the Pharisees.

Conclusion: the cuckoo and the fledgling

In this chapter we have sought to provide two rival accounts of sexuality within the Christian tradition. The dominant account has seen sex as an evil necessitated by the need for procreation. Yet this idea that procreation is the sole legitimate purpose of sexual intercourse is not an inherently Christian one, rather it is a 'cuckoo in the nest', having its origins in a Stoic view of the world rooted in the austere patriarchalism of the Roman Empire. Integral to such sexual pessimism is fear of the danger of emotional contamination with the social inferior 'other half' of the species. In such a view the meaning ascribed to sexuality is reduced either negatively to 'mere pleasure', or to its most obvious of biological functions, procreation. This schizoid mindset still lurks in the hearts and minds of many religious people (including, it would appear, John Paul II) shaping their unquestioned assumptions about sexuality and generating levels of anxiety about the subject so characteristic as to make it one of the identifying hallmarks of Christian communities today. And indeed such a false dichotomy is notably enshrined in official Roman Catholic thinking about contraception, which treats the sexual dimension of the marriage relationship as if it were a sequence of isolated acts of sexual union. This depersonalising of sexual encounter is insulting to faithful married couples seeking to follow in the Christian way and untrue to their experience.

Modern Christian thinkers have, then, been right to embrace the insights into the biology and psychology of human sexuality that has developed in the twentieth century.

Psychology aside, even at the basic level of anatomy and physiology it is no longer plausible to evoke the 'natural' as a category of moral reasoning supportive of procreation as the sole biological function of sex. As a result, a more positive attitude towards the body and sexuality has arisen, which locates sexual intercourse firmly in the context of a relationship of personal love. Such an exalted role for sexual intercourse is not unknown within the Christian tradition, as the writings of two married bishops, Julian of Eclanum and Jeremy Taylor, separated by over a thousand years bears witness. Indeed, it constitutes a long-overdue return for the natural fledgling which was edged out of the nest early in Christian history, namely the foundational idea of man and woman becoming 'one flesh', a spiritual and physical union. Whilst not naïve about the dangers inherent in sexuality and eroticism, this essentially Jewish view underpins the understanding of both Jesus and Paul.

Such an account which privileges the emotional content of marriage and makes a positive evaluation of sexuality as an integral part of interpersonal love is dependent upon a much more exalted role for woman than the weight of Christian tradition has envisaged. As the outstanding Mexican poet and thinker Octavio Paz puts it, in his discussion of the complex interaction between sex, love and eroticism: 'There is no love without feminine freedom.'[29] Greater mutuality and reciprocity between the sexes is then potentially one of the benefits as we seek to exorcise the Stoic ghost which has haunted the Christian tradition, bred fear and anxiety and, I would argue, distorted our attitudes to sex.

If Christians should think of sexual intercourse primarily, but not exclusively, as an expression of a relationship, rather than as an act which potentially bears consequences, the conception of a child, how are we to evaluate when a relationship becomes a suitable context for sexual expression to take place? Traditionally for Christians this has been with the onset of marriage. Before we consider whether this should still be the case we need to ask a more fundamental question: how and when do Christians believe a marriage is initiated?

CHAPTER THREE

Just like everyone else

For the Christian, the issue of cohabitation between a man and a woman must be approached from the perspective of an understanding of marriage. Unlike the sacraments of baptism or holy communion, Christians have tended to see marriage in a wider perspective as rooted in the human pair-bond, as a 'gift of God in creation' or as the *Book of Common Prayer* has it: ' . . . an honourable estate, instituted of God in the time of man's innocency.' Marriage may be 'adorned by Christ' through his presence at the wedding in Cana of Galilee, its nature may be understood in light of Christ's words, for example those concerning divorce, or it may be deepened by theological accounts such as that of Saint Augustine. Yet it remains the case that there is not, in any fundamental sense, something called 'Christian marriage', only ' . . . a reality secular in origin which has acquired a deeper meaning.'[1]

In this chapter I shall argue that the meaning of marriage and discerning when a marriage begins is not as straight-forward as is often assumed. The purpose and shape of the marriage relationship cannot be separated from its wider social context, and so inevitably in what follows there will be a consideration of the ways in which traditional customs and state legislation, formulated to regulate issues of social status, property and inheritance have influenced the received Christian understanding of marriage. One clear example concerns our 'commonsense knowledge' of when a marriage begins: for what we might call the 'ceremonial theory' of marriage as a state that is initiated by a legal act, or even by the public exchange of rings and vows within a church, dates from the late-eighteenth century and is inextricably linked to the emerging bureaucratic needs of a nation in the throes of industrial revolution. In terms of the Christian tradition, such an understanding is best described as an exception to the rule. Before our modern period there existed within the Christian nation of Britain a 'bewildering variety of ways'[2] that marriage could be entered – not unlike the situation today, dominated as it is by the 'untidiness' of contemporary cohabitation.

A natural institution?

Before turning to the Bible, to Christ or to the Church's authority, Christians make an *a priori* claim for marriage, the union of one man and one woman, as in some sense a natural institution. In so doing they are of course in the good company of many philosophical and religious traditions and individuals, including Aristotle:

> The love between husband and wife is evidently a natural feeling, for Nature has made man even more a pairing than a political animal in so far as the family is an older and more fundamental thing than the state ... human beings cohabit not only to get children but to provide whatever is necessary to a fully formed life.[3]

Such a 'natural' understanding was shared by the Greco-Roman civilisation into which Christianity was born. It lay at the heart of the Roman idea of marriage. So, for example, the influential Roman jurist, Ulpian (AD 170–228), in his *Institutes*, recognises that marriage is a human institution, yet one which springs from natural law:

> The natural law is that which nature has taught to all animals ... From this comes the union of a man and a

woman that we call matrimony, and the procreation and rearing of children.[4]

Furthermore, the Roman jurists elaborated upon the 'natural feeling' between husband and wife and explicitly identified it as an integral part of that union, its 'glue', enshrining marital concord or affection (*maritalis affectio*) as a conception of legal significance.

Historical diversity

There are, however, problems with this presumption of marriage as a natural condition: when we talk of 'marriage' are we referring to the same 'thing' across time and space? Is there really, as Aristotle asserts, a natural feeling of 'love between husband and wife'? After all, many marriages, across cultures and through history, have been arranged. They are entered upon not for 'love', but for reasons of policy and pragmatism.

An awareness of the dangers of assuming that we are dealing with the 'same thing' across time is central to the argument of this book, for marriage must be seen to possess a real historicity: 'Marriage should not be construed as an essential, timeless, and unchanging or biologically determined entity.'[5] The lived reality of marriage for men and women in the third century is radically different from that of their descendants of the sixteenth or twenty-first centuries for the simple reason that the social, economic and political contingencies of the historical periods are radically different. Marriages are not formed in a vacuum. We need, then, to understand the past and be attentive to differences in practice and the reasons for these differences, otherwise we will simply enshrine as a timeless norm some 'golden age' that never was and fail to articulate with clarity a coherent and realistic vision for the present.

For some, the geographical and historical diversity is such as to make theological talk of a natural and universal social institution called 'marriage' nonsensical. Clearly there are huge differences between societies in terms of the strength and nature of the bond between husbands and wives, especially in relation to wider kin, the nurture of children, patterns of inheritance or the status of women. Such cultural diversity is significant and beyond dispute yet, without denying the great diversity in forms of marriage across time and space, I would like to suggest that the idea of a pair-bonded union between a man and a woman, commonly referred to as 'marriage' can be seen as a quasi-universal.[6] Whilst the rhetoric of 'arranged' marriages is radically different from that of the 'love' marriages of today – the reality is not *as* divergent as it might first appear. Arranged marriages with suitable spouses of similar standing are not usually forced marriages, even in the most patriarchal of societies, like Ancient Rome. Indeed, there is an extensive literature in many cultures warning parents against harsh and mercenary attitudes to their children's matches, and the right of refusal on the part of the couple is often enshrined in custom and practice. Conversely, practical considerations lie very close to the surface where 'love' is the explicit rationale. Studies of contemporary Western relationships demonstrate that love is very far from blind, and that a pronounced tendency towards 'homogamy' (marriage between people from a similar educational, class and religious background) is a key characteristic. And indeed, rather than 'love' being cited as the primary reason for marriage, one excellent study of newlyweds in Britain in the 1980s found, that:

> The desire to be recognised as a normal independent adult and to secure the future, appears to be the most common motive for marriage.[7]

Nevertheless there are those historians that have sought to

make strong claims about the effects of social change in the early modern period upon various aspects of family life. Phillippe Ariès has written of the 'invention of childhood', Edward Shorter of the development of mourning behaviour and most pertinently in this regard, Lawrence Stone, of the growth of affection for spouses.[8] Writing of the family in early sixteenth-century England, Stone comments:

> . . . relations within the nuclear family, between husband and wife and parents and children, were not much closer than those with neighbours, with relatives, or with 'friends' . . . So far as society was concerned, it was a convenient way of channelling the powerful but potentially disruptive instinct of sexual desire – which it was assumed could be satisfied by any reasonably presentable member of the other sex – and it made possible the production and rearing of legitimate children.[9]

Without wishing to underplay the profound social change of the early modern period, it is likely that such assessments are exaggerated and caricature the emotional landscape of our forebears. Without a doubt there are differences in emphasis in the expression of emotion or in the way that death, marriage or childhood is conceived, but as the social anthropologist, Jack Goody, possibly the greatest contemporary authority on comparative kinship and marriage points out ' . . . emotions are poor material for historians who are likely to make untold mistakes in assessing them.'[10] Inevitably then, a balance has to be struck in any historical account of marriage between the inherent continuities and the ways in which these are shaped by different times and places.

Marriage 'in Christ'

Marriage in Christian understanding is, then, rooted in a claim about the 'naturalness' of the human pair-bond, a claim which is defensible, but not uncontested. Its theological elaboration encapsulated in Christian terminology in the idea of the 'one flesh' presents the ideal, and the real possibility of a permanent, sexually exclusive and harmonious relationship between a man and woman within which children are reared, nurtured and loved. Such a theology strives to furnish an account of the man–woman relationship in relation to God and the created order which promotes human flourishing. Clearly, human beings find permanence, sexual faithfulness and harmony between a particular man and woman a demanding or 'high' vocation, and indeed, no other faith has articulated a more demanding marital discipline. Nevertheless, whilst it is to be hoped that living 'in Christ' will have a profound effect upon married life, marriage does not 'belong' exclusively to Christians and at a fundamental level of understanding there is no theology of Christian marriage, only a Christian theology of marriage.[11]

However, the manner in which marriages are formed, regulated or authorised by a particular society is, in light of factors like property transmission and inheritance, I would argue, a secondary issue and requires a degree of flexible responsiveness, a certain cultural fine tuning, on the part of Christian theologians.

The contemporary Church of England, in common with most churches, 'makes' marriages in 'short liturgical bursts,' that is, generally, in half an hour on a Saturday afternoon in the summer – generally (despite the liturgical provisions) in isolation from the gathered Christian community. Clearly, a complete Christian understanding of the most significant day in many people's lives is not exhausted by this treatment of marriage as a single 'quasi-magical legal event'.[12] Nevertheless, for the majority of people, an understanding of what the Church has to say about marriage is communicated by, but often limited to, such 'liturgical bursts'. The obvious difficulty with this situation is that such occasions, important though they may be, are disconnected from the ongoing social, economic and psychological processes that constitute the reality of becoming married. In this, however, the modern understanding of the formation of marriage as initiated by a single event, what might be called *the ceremonial theory*, is in many ways historically atypical. There is, I would suggest, strong evidence for a good deal of fluidity in marriage practices throughout the Christian period – an inevitable reflection of the ways in which marriage has been culturally shaped by the many dimensions of human societies. Through its current practice, the Church too often reflects back to the wider society an inadequate and abstracted understanding of marriage, remote from the experiential reality.

Before we turn to explore this last claim in more detail, it is worth turning back to consider how Christians have entered upon the 'union of one man with one woman'.

Inheriting custom and practice

Clearly, the first Christians did not invent their marriage customs, laws and practices, rather they inherited them, primarily, but not exclusively, from the milieu of Greco-Roman culture and from their Jewish background. As the second-century writer Athenagoras put it, members of the early Christian community simply 'married like everyone else'. Naturally, then, Christians engaged in a diversity of marriage practices reflecting regional and local difference, and, as importantly, differences in status within communities.

What distinguished the nature of marriage for believers was simply that it took place between baptised people; what distinguished its character was that such marriages were conducted 'in a Christian spirit'. There is little reference in early Christian texts to the institutional dimension of marriage; rather it is the content of marriage that is focused upon. The primary differences between the Christian and the pagan lay with a distinctive ethical conduct: from the outset, the Church placed particular stress on sexual fidelity amongst men, unlike their contemporaries, and took a harder line on divorce than either Jewish or Roman society and, with what might be described as a marital spirituality, espoused the theological analogy Christ/Church: Husband/Wife with the admonition to men that they should ' . . . love their wives as their own bodies' (Eph. 5:28a). Despite our modern misgivings about inequality between the sexes, in historical terms this presents a very 'high' standard for marital life.

Theology is important, but we must be careful not to draw too sharp a line between Christian and pagan practice based solely on the writings of certain highly educated Christian men. First of all there is no doubt that many 'ordinary' Christians did not attain the heights prescribed by the theologians and second, much of the writing about pagan practice has a distinctly polemical quality characteristic of certain Christian writers. In fact in the second century AD the Roman Empire witnessed a certain shift in its moral sensibilities, with a greater emphasis being placed on restraint in sexual matters and a sense of harmony (*concordia*) between husband and wife. The historian Judith Evans Grubbs paints the following picture based on the letters of Pliny:

> Carefully arranged marriages in which the moral qualities of both parties are taken into account reveal an ideal of marriage as a well-planned partnership intended to produce children to whom moral values as well as family name and property are to be transmitted. Adultery and sexual unchastity are abhorrent and shameful to all parties concerned, and subject to legal penalties.[13]

At the beginning of the Christian period, marriage has to be understood in the context of the developed agrarian society of the Mediterranean world. Here, marriage was deeply embedded in and determined by the structures of kinship and politics. Three features appear to have been normative for marriage across the region in the first century: (i) that marriage was a family affair arranged by parents; (ii) usually preceded by betrothal, and (iii) that the initiation of marriage was celebrated in a domestic context presided over by the head of the household, usually the groom's father. This was true for both of the two cultural traditions, the Jewish and the Roman, that influenced the subsequent development and consolidation of theological ideas about marriage in the Middle Ages. From the Jewish background (and the scriptures) medieval Christians elaborated ideas about the significance of betrothal and inherited the notion that consummation initiated marriage, whereas the principle of mutual consent was a bequest of Roman law. In both cases it is crucial to understand the context from which these ideas emerged.

The Jewish understanding

According to Jewish *halakhah* (the traditional texts dealing with law and ritual) the process of getting married was initiated by a betrothal (lit: a 'consecration'), at which the boy and girl were dedicated to each other and the *mohar* (bride-price) was given to the girl's father by the prospective husband. The Rabbinic sources then prescribe a year-long betrothal period followed by the nuptials, *kiddushin* ('the sanctification') which ended with a week-long wedding feast, during which a series of seven benedictions were recited by the father of the groom. After this the groom led the bride to his house, or more properly the bridal chamber (*huppah*) to consummate the marriage.

It is axiomatic, then, to traditional Jewish understanding

that marriage is begun when sexual intercourse has taken place, or at least presumed to have occurred. Such practice places the initiation of sexual union at the heart of the marriage process and brings betrothal closer to the status of an unconsummated marriage than a prospective agreement.[14] Indeed, Rabbinic law recognises that, whilst less than ideal, sexual intercourse is one valid way of establishing a betrothal (*Mishnah Ket* 4.4). However, even within Israel there seems to have been differences in local practice. Whilst in Galilee, a betrothed girl would remain *virgo intacta* in her father's house, the evidence from the *Mishnah* and other records strongly suggest that pre-marital cohabitation (and sexual activity) was practised with some regularity in Judea.[15]

Mediterranean culture

One of the key elements in traditional marriage settlements within the cultural sphere of the Mediterranean world was the presentation by the prospective bridegroom of a pre-nuptial gift to the bride's family. Such gifts, like those flowing in the other direction – the dowry – acted as insurance policies, not unlike contemporary pre-nuptial agreements. For whilst the pre-nuptial gift remained under the husband's control during marriage, it was forfeited if he divorced his wife without good cause and it was retained by her after his death. In addition, however, such pre-nuptial gifts were seen as a compensation for the loss of a girl's virginity.

This premium on female chastity in Mediterranean culture has to be understood in the context of the deeply entrenched and pervasive cultural values associated with honour and shame. The honour/shame system is characteristic of societies in which the dominant social (and political) relationships are those between fathers and sons, and between related males more broadly. Here there is a premium on expressions of male solidarity within families and competition between families which has a profound influence on sexuality and the relationship between the sexes. Central to this is the idea of honour, the esteem a (male) person has within their own eyes in conjunction with the acceptance of that valuation by their male kin group. Honour is demonstrated in the public domain through a range of behaviour demonstrating male autonomy and authority *vis-a-vis* men from other kin-groups. It is this striving for, and maintaining of honour that constitutes the 'plague' on 'both the houses' of Capulet and Montague in Shakespeare's *Romeo and Juliet*. Honour is therefore a competitive notion and failure in some regard brings, in its wake – shame. One dimension to the achievement of family honour is the reciprocal relationship between men and women: the more that women, who are often perceived to be morally inferior in such a system, exhibit modesty and engage in appropriate acts of social deference, the greater is the honour that reflects upon 'their' men. Conversely, the more men display autonomy and mastery in the public realm, the greater the reflected esteem upon female members of the family.[16] However if, for example, a young man acts violently or inappropriately in public, or a girl is seduced, such actions reflect directly on the head of the household and bring him dishonour. Such ideas with their evaluations of the nature of men and women had a profound influence on the way in which marriage was conceived within the first-century Greco-Roman world into which Christianity emerged.

Legislating for marriage: citizens and concubines

In turning from a consideration of Jewish to Roman ideas of marriage, we are brought from the world of custom and practice into one in which state legislation begins to have a distinctive role. Indeed, many contemporary legal ideas and practices can be traced back to Roman predecessors. However, in considering the important role of legislation, we must begin by drawing two central distinctions.

The first is that modern legal conceptions of marriage, in continuity with ecclesiastical ideas, assume that to get married is to take on a 'set of obligations that are defined and enforced by law,'[17] By contrast, legislation crafted for the Roman Empire was concerned only with the *legal consequences of marriage* – namely issues concerned with inheritance and social status. The overwhelming significance of marriage lay with the fact that only children born of such a union were considered legitimate heirs. In Roman eyes so long as a couple regarded each other as man and wife and others perceived that to be the case, then they were considered to be married. Marriage was simply a given, a matter of fact, its nature neither defined nor reflected upon.

The second is that whilst we tend to assume that marriage is a fundamental institution of society that is available to all who wish to enter, within the Roman Empire it was a highly exclusive institution restricted to certain social classes. Consciousness of status pervaded the Roman culture and this was reflected in the legislation which attempted to maintain clear demarcations between various social groups. Perhaps the clearest example of this can be found in the Augustan marriage legislation, *Lex Julia de maritandis ordinibus* (18 BC) in which the marriage of the upper classes (senatorial families) with freed persons (or actors) was strictly forbidden. Not only was formal marriage a restricted institution, but it was also an institution central to the maintenance of the hierarchical and coercive power of an empire built upon the sweat and blood of slaves. Religious authority in Roman society was vested in the *paterfamilias*, the male head of the household and, to a proportionately greater degree, in the Emperor, whose semi-divine status generated cultic practices that it was difficult for conscientious Christians to follow. The *concordia*, the mutual affection between the Emperor and his wife, was thus regarded as a model for the 'harmony' of Roman rule. It is not hard to see that under such circumstances the early Christian communities scattered throughout the Mediterranean could be perceived with justification to be opposed to 'family values', for as sisters and brothers 'in Christ' they proclaimed a radically new 'family' within which there was in some sense 'neither Jew nor Greek, male nor female, slave nor free' (Gal. 3:28).

Roman marriage legislation varied over the early Christian centuries affecting the proportion of the population eligible for legal marriage (*iustum matrimonium*). However, in addition to such unions, we might recognise two other basic forms of a 'union between a man and a woman' that were, at the very least marriage-like: the *contubernia* (quasi-marital relationships) and *concubinatus* (concubinage).

The dominant manifestation of legal marriage in the early Christian period was known as 'free marriage'. Although a woman took her husband's rank on marriage, she did not become part of her husband's family, rather she remained under the authority of her own *paterfamilias*, usually her father. In such a marriage, few obligations were placed upon a spouse in relation to their partner. Whilst the legislation governing formal marriage varied over the early Christian period, its essence can be best understood in relation to two central ideas – *conubium* and *consensus*. *Conubium* is the legal capacity of a couple to marry. In addition to the restrictions that we might anticipate (that people could not marry before puberty or marry someone who was closely related) there were a number of other preconditions to be met relating to citizenship and social status. Assuming that the state of *conubium* existed between a couple, what then made marriage in Roman law was very simple – agreement (*consensus*), that is the agreement of the couple themselves and that of the *paterfamilias*, the head (or even ruler) of the respective households – usually the father.

Legal marriage (*iustum matrimonium*) was then essentially an informal union. By custom, the process of getting married was begun by betrothal (*sponsolia*) – a public agreement to marry in the future entered into by the *paterfamilias* after protracted negotiations and determination of the suitability of the young people in question. Evidence suggests that Roman men tended to marry in their late twenties and women a decade earlier. Whilst the girl's consent was required, age, custom and considerations of female modesty and propriety conspired to make her involvement rather passive, whereas prospective husbands often had a role in the negotiations. When a suitable match between families of equal social standing, wealth and birth had been arranged, the *sponsalia* was characteristically celebrated with a party. Prior to this party, the couples might exchange gifts and the prospective husband would send his intended a ring as a pledge. Similarly dowries and counter-dowries were exchanged with regularity, though often to ensure clarity that a marriage (*iustum matrimonium*) was intended rather than concubinage. It was also commonplace from the first century onwards to draw up a document that was signed and witnessed. Indeed, towards the end of the period, in AD 538, a rule was introduced that for all but the lowest classes, a marriage could not be considered valid without such clear documentary evidence of *concensus*. However, none of these ceremonies, gift-givings or documents in and of themselves related to the legitimacy of the union *per se* – *consensus* alone was the criteria.

In Roman law then, marriage was considered legal if the couple consented and there were no legal impediments to the union. Furthermore, if a couple were living together between whom *conubium* existed, they were considered to be married with their cohabitation being taken as evidence of *consensus*. It is crucial here to grasp that the Roman idea of *consensus* was not, as it was subsequently understood to be, 'an initial act of agreement creating a continuing and binding obligation', but a 'continuing condition, so that a marriage would last as long as there was consensus and would cease when consensus ceased.'[18] The existence of a marriage was thus dependent on continuing marital accord. Indeed, it could be argued that the subsequent Christian emphasis on the initial act of 'getting married', a result of developing theological ideas about the nature of marriage, has led regrettably to a reduced emphasis on the experience of being married.

Although unable to enter into official recognised marriages, the freed classes and the extensive slave population, who made up one-third of the society, also aspired to live together in permanent unions in which they could raise children. Such quasi-marital relationships (*contubernia*) varied immensely in form, but those who entered them sought to appropriate the reality and ' . . . the terminology of legal marriage'[19] to describe their relationships. However, many did so in the face of severe constraints, for, as property rather persons, slaves could be sold at whim and it was perfectly acceptable for a slave-owner to have sexual access to his slaves. Such brute facts of life inevitably disrupted the informal unions (*contubernia*) that slaves were able to form. In addition to such unions being forcibly ended by the sale of one slave, they could also be forcibly initiated by a slave-owner with an eye to economic gain (i.e. slave children). Under such conditions in which the principles of animal husbandry were forced upon powerless, isolated and degraded men and women, the 'goods' of marriage, as Christians have understood them – permanence, exclusivity and children – would have been all too frequently beyond the reach of many.

The third category of monogamous union is usually called *concubinatus*. Such a union was not what we usually think of as concubinage – a secondary relationship 'on the side' – in addition to marriage. Rather, *concubinatus* as a category of relationship was effectively created by the marriage legislation of the Emperor Augustus (63 BC–AD 14). This legislation attempted to shore up the position of the Roman aristocracy and included pro-natalist policies alongside tighter restrictions on who could marry whom, designed to preserve the integrity of the aristocratic class. As a result the number of relationships occurring between people whose divergent social status precluded the possibility of formal marriage (and therefore legitimate heirs) increased. Such monogamous (and potentially lifelong) relationships were often entered into by older men who had no desire for more legitimate heirs, or by younger men, not yet ready for a legal marriage and legitimate offspring. Perhaps the most famous example of such a relationship is that between Augustine and his unnamed lover of 17 years. Here the picture painted is of a socially acceptable monogamous, sexual relationship between a man and a woman who is his social inferior. Equally acceptable, in its day, was its termination with the prospect for Augustine of a legitimate marriage with a more suitable mate.

The character of this unequal yoking evolved from era to era in response to changing legislation and social conventions. So in the fourth and fifth centuries, *concubinatus* clearly existed between couples who did possess the legal right to marry; what was 'missing' was then quite simply the intention, the *consensus*, of the man in question. This changed the essential character of the relationship, in effect making it an alternative to full marriage.

Although the Church made some efforts to appropriate concubinage to the institution of marriage, in practice it recognised the difference between the two and exhibited an extraordinary degree of toleration to such a union over a considerable period. Concubinage existed as a significant social phenomenon well into the Middle Ages – indeed clerical concubinage provided a semi-official solution to the problems generated by 'clerical celibacy' until after the Gregorian reforms of the eleventh century.

From secular to sacred

Unless they involved sacrifices to pagan gods or other acts of idolatry, early Christians throughout the Roman Empire tended to follow local marriage customs. So, for example, in a brief discussion of marriage liturgy, Clement of Alexandria (c. 150–215) strongly implies a continuity with Jewish traditions and includes a clear reference to the traditional blessing of the couple. His near-contemporary Tertullian (c. 160–220), on the other hand, presupposes a number of elements central to Roman practice (and indeed familiar to us): the bridal veil, the giving of a ring, the custom of the bridal kiss and of the joining of hands accompanying the giving of consent. Occasionally, the practices of other Christians raised alarm bells. Tertullian, for example, condemns unequivocally as pagan the Roman practice of crowning the husband and wife with garland-crowns. Yet such a practice was common in the eastern Mediterranean and has remained central to the marriage liturgies of the Orthodox churches. There are a few hints of distinctively Christian conventions emerging, the earliest, in one of the epistles of Ignatius (AD 110), suggests that the bishop may take the traditional role of the Roman pater or Jewish father in giving permission for a marriage to take place, perhaps even in blessing it:

> It is right for men and women who marry to establish their union with the approval of the bishop that the marriage may be according to the Lord.[20]

However, although it became customary for a priest to bless Christian couples from the fourth century in some parts of the Empire, there is no unambiguous evidence of an explicit and distinctive Christian wedding ceremony until well into the medieval period.[21]

Over the centuries of the first millennium however, with the growing power and influence of the Church, a gradual shift took place, with the secular and domestic emphasis giving way to the sacred and ecclesial. With the more expansive jurisdiction of the Church in the early Middle Ages came a pressing need to define when a marriage existed, and when it did not, so that legal conflicts over property and inheritance could be resolved. With its dual inheritance from Roman and Jewish culture, the Church faced, and sought to resolve, a certain degree of tension between the bequests of the 'will' and the 'flesh', the emphasis on consent within Roman law and sexual consummation within Judaism. Many attempts to resolve this tension between whether it was consent or consummation were made during the patristic and medieval periods. One moderately successful attempt by the theologian Tertullian is illustrative of the way in which theological and legal perspectives on marriage were resolved. It focuses on the fact that 'a kiss' is not always *just* a kiss'.

In his discussion of the status of the betrothed woman, Tertullian presupposes that it is customary to confirm a betrothal with a kiss and the joining of hands. A striking feature of his discussion is the emphasis that the theologian places on becoming: getting married, for Tertullian, was a process of fulfilment, of realisation, with the clear *terminus ad quem* – the union of the two in the one flesh. Yet Tertullian considered that a betrothed woman was in a spiritual sense already married, already in an anticipated sense belonging to her husband, being halfway along the path from the potential to the actual. Tertullian therefore attaches particular importance to the 'betrothal kiss' as a symbol of the consummation that is to follow in time. He was not alone. The centrality of this betrothal kiss was subsequently underlined by a law of Constantine of AD 336 in which it was put forward that if a betrothed person should die, half of the betrothal gift should be returned if the kiss had occurred and all of it if it had not.

Similarly, the earliest disciplinary laws associated with marriage, the canons of the Council of Elvira (c. AD 300) decreed that parents who broke off a betrothal should be excommunicated for three years unless either the man or woman had committed some grave offence. However, if the couple themselves had sexually anticipated their marriage, the betrothal could not be broken off by the parents. Even at this early stage the desire to bring consummation close to betrothal, the point at which consent is pledged, can be clearly seen.

Betrothal and sexual consummation must then be seen as 'correlative' terms, that is, betrothal looks forward to consummation, whilst consummation fulfils betrothal. It would seem, then, that once a betrothal had been confirmed by the joining of the hands and the seal of the kiss, it was regarded as a solemn and binding contract, as a kind of virtual but unratified marriage. Philip Reynolds summarises the situation in the early Middle Ages:

> [G]etting married was a process rather than a simple act. The spouses initiated their marriage by their betrothal and they consummated it by sexual intercourse. Other elements, such as customs of courtship and the nuptial liturgy, might occur at various points between these terms or before the betrothal. The state of the partners after their betrothal but before they began to live together or before they consummated their marriage was intermediate and in some respects uncertain, for they were neither single nor married.[22]

A 'rite of passage'

Entry to marriage continued to be seen as a process which in addition to generating a growing body of legislation also led to the elaboration of various liturgical forms which incorporated and sacralised regional customs. Unlike other forms of social action designed to communicate and effect change (like legislation) such rituals provide a symbolic and embodied form of social knowing that is highly effective in restructuring the landscape of the everyday, transforming both individuals and the ways in which they are perceived. Men and women are socially reborn through ritual and recognised afresh as a consequence of it.

One of the more robust insights from the human sciences concerns the manner in which societies handle fundamental changes in status, often associated with biological change (birth, puberty, marriage, death, etc). In his classic study *Les rites de passage* published in 1908, the Dutch anthropologist, Arnold van Gennep, analysed such transitions and suggested that they were facilitated by the same basic threefold process involving rites of separation, of preparation and of incorporation. In the first stage, the individual or class of individuals is separated out from 'their world' and marked for future change. In so doing they enter a state 'betwixt and between' marked by confusion and readjustment in which those involved are of ambivalent social status. This period of liminality is only resolved through rites of incorporation which acknowledge the new status of the individual undergoing the transition. Such a threefold structure appears to hold true cross-culturally and may well reflect the basic human socio-psychological needs that we have, as embodied rational creatures, for time and space in which to come to terms with a transformed reality.

This threefold pattern is readily illustrated in traditional societies by the transition from the single to the married state. Characteristically, there is a preliminary and provisional commitment at what is often termed betrothal when the couple are marked off from the world of youth and start to re-orientate themselves to the status of married adulthood as they and the community accept the interim commitment to marry at some point in the future. Following this initial commitment, in the liminal stage, the couple prepare for the duties and responsibilities of married adulthood, whilst the families, kin and peer groups of each party to the alliance enter a relationship marked by increasing commitment and nego-tiation of both a personal and economic nature (with attendant tensions). Finally, the rite of marriage incorporates the couple into the world of married adults – often through a shared meal dependent on the final economic transaction (dowry, bridewealth, etc). Consummation, and to a lesser extent, co-residence may occur at any point following the initial rite of betrothal through to the final rite of marriage.

In his account of the history of Christian marriage liturgies, Kenneth Stevenson argues that betrothal and the 'in-between' stage it initiated 'was an essential part in the process of getting married as a Christian'[23] throughout the first Christian millen-nium. Indeed, he goes on to demonstrate this, through an account of the variety of ways in which churches ritualised the separation rites involved in betrothal. Furthermore, he draws attention to those ecclesial traditions in which the period of liminality was itself ritualised. So, for example, following a betrothal liturgy we have the blessing of wedding robes in the Coptic Church, the Armenian blessing of the marriage chamber, and the use of the liturgy of the hours in the Visigothic rite.

Whilst this intermediate period, begotten of community and custom, fulfilled an important social and psychological function, the inherent uncertainty did not help the dilemmas of the lawyers. Over time, as the principle of consent was clearly enshrined in canon law, it led inevitably to the end of distinct betrothal rites. Even where they survived in some vestigial form they became assimilated into the same liturgical structure as marriage, focusing on question and consent and upon priestly formulae. The distinctive contribution and sig-nificance of betrothal as a part of the Christian understanding of marriage was forgotten. With this development came an increased focus on the marriage service itself, not primarily as the occasion upon which a couple were blessed, but at which they exchanged consent. This process culminated in the decision of the Roman Catholic Church at the Council of Trent (1563), that a marriage was only truly valid in the eyes of the Church if it took place in front of a priest in a wedding ceremony.

Sex and betrothal in early modern England

By the time of this further extension of the Church's control, much of northern Europe had already undergone the Reformation, and the principle that marriage was constituted by the mutual consent of the couple in question was enshrined in the customs and practices of the newly Protestant countries. Furthermore, whilst its ritualisation by the Church may have receded, the practice of betrothal was thriving. From the sixteenth to the early nineteenth century in Britain a clear understanding that mutual consent made a marriage lay at the heart of a plurality of informal marriage customs which reflected or represented a range of different interests (property, kinship, etc) and enshrined the practical morality of local communities.[24] Betrothal was chief among such customs. The social historian John Gillis describes it as possessing great strategic significance in the politics of courtship and marriage, a recognised rite of transition which conferred on the couple the right to sexual as well as social intimacy:

> Betrothal granted freedom to explore for any personal faults or incompatibilities that had remained hidden during the earlier, more inhibited phases of courtship and could be disastrous if carried into the indissoluble status of marriage.[25]

The patristic and medieval understanding of betrothal was as a binding contract which carried penalties for those who broke it and within which any children born would be counted among the illegitimate. Betrothal in early modern England as it was commonly practised, on the other hand, could be dissolved by either party within the first year, unless the woman was pregnant, and any children born before marriage were considered legitimate. Describing the situation at the turn of the nineteenth century, Gillis writes:

> Sexual intimacy was normal once marriage had been promised ... Couples might set a date and then, for no fault of their own, see it pass, with the woman pregnant or the child already born ... There was little shame attached to premarital pregnancy and couples tended to put off the marriage ceremony until a time economically convenient for both parties.[26]

Such widespread acceptance of sexual intimacy prior to a full commitment to permanence reflected a significant cultural shift, in which the affections and will of the couple progressively displaced the establishment of alliances between families, and the role that issues like property and inheritance played in the decision to marry was accompanied by a weakening of the link between sexual pleasure and sin. This shift continued with the urbanisation of Britain resulting from the profound economic change associated with the Industrial Revolution.

The Hardwicke Act, 1753, and the 'ceremonial theory'

The modern understanding of marriage is rooted in the Hardwicke Act of 1753 which made its public registration mandatory. This legislation marked a watershed in marriage formation and established, in its long wake, what might be termed the 'ceremonial theory of marriage'; that is that marriages are 'made' rather than *solemnised* by a half-hour religious service on a Saturday afternoon. In its day however, the introduction of compulsory registration of marriage, criminalising private marriage-making, was seen by many as a gross infringement of personal liberties. As Horace Walpole recorded in his memoirs:

> It was amazing in a country where liberty gives choice, where trade and money confer equality, and where facility of marriage has always been supposed to produce populousness – it was amazing to see a law promulgated that cramped inclination, that discountenanced matrimony, and that seemed to annex as sacred privileges to birth, as could be devised in the proudest, poorest little Italian principality.[27]

Ironically, for a piece of innovative legislation which had a quite 'modern' feel, the proponents of the Hardwicke Act were desperately trying to preserve some decidedly 'old world' values. Driven through parliament by the aristocrats of the Upper House, which had failed on no fewer than seven earlier occasions to pass similar legislation, the main motivation was to prevent hasty (and unsuitable) matches and thereby protect the inheritance of wealth and property in times of unprecedented social mobility, and the increasing popularity of romantic love as a basis for a more companionate marriage. Whilst the Church of England became an integral part of the registration system following the Act, it was primarily a piece of legislation which ceded power from the individual to the State.

Informal marriage practices continued well into the nineteenth century and estimates suggest that one in five couples had experienced cohabitation outside of marriage between 1750 and 1850.[28] However, from the 1840s there was greater bureaucratic efficiency, most pertinently in the registration of marriage following the Civil Marriage Act of 1836, and enhanced transport and communication infrastructure binding communities more firmly into an increasingly cohesive national life, combined with a fierce moralistic opposition to the pluralistic and informal marriage practices of the working classes on the part of the rising Victorian middle class. The status of 'married respectability' emerged as a powerful vehicle of public virtue and orderliness in a culture increasingly dominated by Evangelical social reformers. Individuals living according to the old ways, along with their officially 'illegitimate' children, experienced stigma and discrimination. This process of encouraging people to marry in a proper and orderly manner continued throughout the twentieth century with a 'tutelary complex' of social workers, educationalists and criminologists, enforcing an increasing uniformity in marriage practice amongst the 'feckless' working class who persisted in 'livin' tally' or 'over t'brush'.

Cohabitation in historical perspective

I suggested at the outset of this chapter that marriage has evolved and changed its shape as an inevitable consequence of profound economic, demographic and social change. That Christian ideas about marriage and its formation should develop from their origins within a largely agrarian society ruled by a semi-divine Emperor and ruthless military machine, economically under-girded by slavery and characterised by high death rates, to a post-industrial democracy with equal rights legislation, universal family planning and high levels of life expectancy is inevitable and appropriate.

The rise of cohabitation over the past twenty years and the ease with which it has become acceptable to the majority of the population should not, then, be interpreted as 'the end of marriage' as some have conceived it, nor as a clear indication of the progressive corrosion of the moral fabric of our society, as others would like to suggest.[29] Rather for most people, ' ... cohabitation is part of the process of getting married and is not a substitute for marriage.'[30] Its popularity is, then, one example among many, of a well-documented and much broader social shift away from institutional authority and towards a reassertion of the personal and the individual. From this perspective it reflects a reassessment of how marriage has been understood in the last two centuries, and a pendulum shift in the balance of power over who has the authority to define marriages, back to a situation similar to that which existed before the civil registration of marriage in 1753. When disillusionment or doubt about marriage as an 'institution' and talk of the marriage licence as 'just a piece of paper' is voiced, it does not, then, constitute a wholesale rejection of a basically Christian understanding of marriage: rather it is, in part, an expression of ambivalence about the role of the state in personal life.

Within the currently evolving situation, an established Church should then be cautious about wedding itself to a temporally 'local' understanding of marriage, which places, historically speaking, undue emphasis on its legal and bureaucratic dimensions. Such an emphasis is open to the interesting criticism that Ford and Hardy level at the contemporary church:

> The nation state is delighted to welcome a religion that is so timid and orderly, leaving the passions free for economics, war, and collective sport. In Britain today the civic religion might be described as stoicism with the Christian influence. It is full of rectitude, good patterns and principles, but it is being challenged by more exciting and extreme creeds to which it seems at present to have neither the daring nor the moral, intellectual and political creativity to respond.[31]

Rather, I would suggest, the Church should embrace the opportunity for a fresh engagement with couples who are seeking to build lives together. It should celebrate their journey into marriage, but also make a serious commitment to accompanying couples in the subsequent life phases of marriage.

One of the unfortunate consequences of the need to define, for legal purposes, the beginning of a marriage has been the loss of the Church's involvement with the domestic rite of betrothal. This has created a tension or distance in post-Reformation Christianity between the 'Church' and the 'home'. A more profound pastoral and liturgical exploration of the process of 'becoming married', reflecting the 'everyday' social and psychological processes in a creative way, might allow for a greater grounding of the Church in the everyday domestic world of the home – what the Church Father, John Chrysostom, conceived of as the 'domestic church'. This could be achieved in a number of ways, for example through the public and ritual acknowledgement of engagement, perhaps coincident with the point at which a couple begin to live together. This would have 'the advantage of spreading the sacrament of marriage over a far wider terrain than it has occupied for many centuries. It could demarginalise our marital practice and rescue it from trivialization.'[32] Whilst this is a possibility and a number of people have called for the reintroduction, in some shape or form, of a betrothal rite, most notably Adrian Thatcher, its popularity in the current climate marked by a significant decline in church weddings seems unlikely. Perhaps a more realistic point of engagement might come in the form of relationship preparation and support.[33]

However, for the Church to return to an historical under-standing of marriage as a staged process in response to cohabitation would require it to accept the fact that the vast majority of reasonable, morally serious young (and not so young) people have initiated a sexual relationship before they wish to make public even a provisional commitment to be together for the rest of their lives. Even if one accepted that a phased approach to marriage might make practical, pastoral, perhaps liturgical sense, surely accepting the possibility of pre-marital sexual intercourse would simply be a fatal concession on the part of the Church to secularising forces, a dilution of its teaching in a culture which 'fosters all kinds of misleading fantasies about sex'.[34] I might concur with this last point were it not for the fact that the Protestant churches have already engaged in a more profound innovation within the Christian tradition which prepared the ground for a new approach to sexuality within society and which necessitates a reassessment, though not a severing of the link between sex and marriage.

CHAPTER FOUR

Ever since the Sixties

The most influential theological text on marriage within the Western tradition is that of Augustine's *De Bono conjugali* (On the Good of Marriage), written in AD 401. In it he turns to consider what the minimum requirements might be for a relationship to constitute a marriage:

> It is often asked whether this situation should be called a marriage: when a man and a woman, neither of whom is married to another, have intercourse with each other, not in order to have children, but out of incontinence solely to have sex and yet faithfully pledge not to do this with anyone else. Perhaps it would not be absurd to call this a marriage, if they made this agreement to last until the death of one of them, and if, although they have not come together for the sake of procreation, they do not at least avoid it, either by not wishing to have children or by acting in an evil way to prevent children being born. But if one or both of these conditions are absent, I do not see how we could call this a marriage.[1]

This is a particularly poignant passage, for Augustine is a man 'with a past'. Fifteen years beforehand he had dismissed the concubine he had lived with faithfully since he was a young man of 18 in order to leave himself free to make a more suitable match. Not only did Augustine choose to end his relationship with this woman, but it was also a relationship which over 13 years had resulted in the birth of a single child, suggestive that he himself had 'taken precautions' to prevent conception.

If we were to subject this extract to the lens of contemporary mores – three differences emerge:

- The first is that the historical Augustine does not share the widespread (Protestant) acceptance of contraception as morally permissible. For Augustine, to deliberately avoid conception is to violate one of the central purposes of marriage and therefore make it a different sort of relationship. Unless, of course, swayed by the arguments of his fellow Christians, a contemporary Augustine would then warm to the language of Pope John Paul II, who has spoken of contraceptive practice as part and parcel of 'a culture of death'.

- The second, is that Augustine, in line with most historical Christians, does not adhere to the modern ceremonial theory of marriage formation, instead he assumes that marriage is made fundamentally by intention and commitment. When a relationship is sexually exclusive and the couple have a shared understanding that the relationship is permanent, a marriage exists – no external validation is required.

- The third and perhaps more pressing issue for the modern mind is one of social justice. The casting aside of a socially inferior faithful lover (whom Augustine never names, but clearly loved) in preparation for a more suitable marriage (which as it happens he never made) strikes us quite powerfully as reprehensible. Yet within the society that Augustine inhabited, founded upon certain hierarchical and patriarchal assumptions, such behaviour was perfectly acceptable. Indeed Augustine's devout Christian mother, Monica, encouraged such a course of action, and as we have noted in the last chapter, the Church did little to challenge the institution of concubinage as a 'second-class marriage' premised on social inequality throughout its first millennia.

Whilst reprehensible to Augustine at a distance of some years, such callous and calculating behaviour in his past would, one suspects, be judged more harshly by the contemporary Church – doubtless lingering long on the files of those responsible for weighing the merits of candidates for the episcopate in the modern Church.

I have opened with this 'compare and contrast' exercise to conjure something of the difference of emphasis that a weighty historical theologian like Augustine brings to the question of when a marriage exists. This provides us with a different vantage point from which to survey the landscape of contemporary relationships and evaluate the emergent practice of cohabitation. For in this chapter, in which we will look at the evolution of the marriage relationship in the twentieth century, it is to these three central and highly interrelated themes, albeit in a radically different social context, that we must turn to consider the reasons for the emergence of widespread cohabitation: the balance between external authorisation (State and Church) and the private individual; the status of women; and the connection between sexuality and procreation. In historical perspective, I shall argue, prompted by Augustine, that it is the ethical acceptability of family limitation and the practice of contraception that constitutes the fundamental break with the authoritative weight of the Christian tradition. Compared with this moral innovation, which I believe we should embrace, the question of cohabitation (with certain caveats) should be considered comparatively minor.

The subsidence of moral certainties

Since the 1960s there has been a significant, even revolutionary shift in sexual, marital and procreative behaviour and attitudes within Britain[2] with the evolution of a mass divorce culture, the postponement of marriage and child-bearing as well as increasing numbers of people entering marriage after a significant period of cohabitation. This 'flight from marriage' can be most clearly illustrated by looking at snapshots a decade apart: in 1971, 81 per cent of women had married by the age of 25, by 1981 this had fallen a little to 71 per cent, but by 1991 it had fallen dramatically to 46 per cent, continuing to fall to 39 per cent in 1996.[3] As a result, the average age at first marriage has risen dramatically, for women, from 21 in 1970 to the historically unprecedented age of 28 in 2001. Divorce, which affected around one in ten couples at the beginning of the 1960s, now ends 40 per cent of marriages.[4] Contemporary family life now has an unprecedented diversity and fluidity to it, with the rhythm of separations and new relationships creating 'patchwork' families, or to change the analogy, rendering to family life the quality of a building site under construction, within which children might experience successively the care of a single parent, the estrangement of a biological parent and the arrival of a step-parent, and have to negotiate relationships with step- or half-siblings and a range of related adults.

Such a radical and swift change in the patterns of relationship formation and dissolution and in the nature of the couple relationship is common to the Western world, albeit with significant regional variations, and could reasonably be described as a 'great disruption' or a 'relationship revolution',[5] a tear in the social fabric. How then is this revolution to be explained and evaluated?

A culture crumbles

For many Christian commentators such rapid change is most frequently viewed negatively as part of a broader narrative of secularisation in which British culture ceases to be defined and structured by a shared moral order rooted in a common

Christian worldview. Rather, with the advent of the so-called 'permissive society', Christian values have been displaced and morality has become deregulated.

Such an analysis makes a good deal of sense. Whilst sociologists have traditionally described secularisation, the decline of religious influence in modern society, as a drawn-out affair, more recent scholars have identified the early sixties as a critical period. In *The Death of Christian Britain*, for example, Callum Brown argues that:

> ... quite suddenly in 1963, something very profound ruptured the character of the nation and its people sending organised Christianity on a downward spiral to the margins of social significance.[6]

Brown's argument is that what we have witnessed in the last few decades is not just a decline in church attendance, but the death of a culture, the demise of Britain's core religious and moral identity: 'the end of Christianity as a means by which men and women, as individuals, construct their identities and their sense of "self".'[7]

Alongside sociologist Grace Davie[8] who describes the 1950s as a thoroughly Anglican decade, Brown points out that in the period 1945–1958 there was a significant increase in several measures of religious behaviour including church and Sunday School attendance. More importantly he argues, people's lives in the 1950s were acutely affected by the symbols, activities and authority of the Church. In an atmosphere of economic and cultural austerity, unprecedented moral concern about delinquency and deviancy was accompanied by an assertion of the virtues of thrift, sexual restraint, duty and respectability, moulding a society which placed a very high value on personal conformity. From the perspective of the family it was a period in which divorce rates plateaued and extramarital childbearing reached an all time low. On the surface, it was, then, a 'golden age' for marriage, in which 'never before had so many married and with such ceremony.'[9]

However, the next decade brought a dramatic cultural revolution and the ' . . . complex web of legally and socially accepted rules which governed individual identity in Christian Britain until the 1950s'[10] was swept away; how people constructed their lives and what constituted the 'good and the bad' changed fundamentally. Lorna Sage, in her auto-biographical account of childhood, captures something of the flavour of such transformation, as it affected even deepest rural Shropshire. Painting a picture of her mother's generation:

> *Bring me my bow of burning gold. Bring me my arrows of desire* sang the WI, dreaming of stainless steel spatulas and electric whisks. Their tweeds smelt of damp and camphor, their jowls trembled under a coating of powder, their lipstick ran up into the cracks under their mous-taches and their blue eyes watered from the fumes of the coke stove. They never took off their hats (felt, feathers) even when they shed their jackets to pass round tea and sandwiches.

She reflects that:

> Rock'n'roll made the separation of generations official, teenagers post 1955 were a tribe apart, they marched to a different rhythm . . . Their fifties was a different place.[11]

Indeed, mention of some of the more prominent events of the period – the 1960 censorship trial of *Lady Chatterley's Lover*, the emergence of the Beatles in October 1962 with the release of 'Love Me Do' and the public ridicule of the establishment in *That Was the Week That Was* – quickly conjure that sense of radical discontinuity in culture. Such events marked a watershed in British social history: the moment when ' . . .

the institutional structures of cultural traditionalism started to crumble.'[12]

The privatisation of morality

This shift in social and moral authority, towards what might be described as a secular individualism, found its most concrete manifestation in the change of attitude towards personal and sexual morality in areas like homosexuality, abortion and divorce. At the beginning of the decade, public legislation was underpinned by a clear moralist stance, that certain acts were wrong, in and of themselves, and that the State had a duty and responsibility to punish transgressors in the name of justice. By the end of the decade this situation had been transformed as a result of changes in social attitudes; legislation grounded in the 'givenness' of traditional Christian teaching was replaced by legislation aimed at minimising harm, pain and suffering. Furthermore, these legislative changes were prompted not primarily by cries for reform from secular humanists, but flowed from considered Christian opinion expressed in a number of influential publications issued by the Church of England.[13]

Such a shift in legislation reflected a broader retreat from narrow confessional authority from the public realm with the responsibility for moral decision-making effectively 'privatised' or 'relocated' to the individual. Whilst this fragmentation of an overarching moral framework within which to make decisions was liberating for many individuals, especially women, and most notably those trapped in 'empty shell' marriages or those leading covert gay lifestyles, such new-found freedom could also be experienced as disorienting. Increasingly, individuals have found themselves condemned to freedom, unsure of what they really want, yet having to ' . . . engage with, a world of plural choices', and having to simply ' . . . opt for alternatives, given that the signposts established by tradition are now blank.'[14] A pertinent example of the difficulties posed by such a privatisation of morality concerns the issue of marital breakdown. The evolution from a system in which 'fault' was assigned by the legal system which identified 'guilty' and 'innocent' parties to one in which 'irretrievable breakdown' became the sole ground for divorce, shifted the burden of deciding whether a marriage had ended and the personal responsibility for the consequences of that decision firmly onto the shoulders of the men and women concerned. One ironic consequence of this shift in meaning was established by the results of a *Conciliation in Divorce* survey conducted in the 1980s:

> The fact is that many people do not know whether their marriage is at end; indeed they may be using the legal process as a way of finding out.[15]

The flight from the institutional

There is no doubt that the 1960s brought about a fundamental shift in the relationship between individuals and traditional forms of authority, whether they were political, religious or legal. The authority of the 'Establishment' was undermined and redefined; it could no longer simply command unquestioning respect. As the nature of such authority was ultimately a moral one, and formed part of an integrated cultural system which was explicitly grounded in a Christian worldview, the diminution of religion's objective taken-for-grantedness and the decline in church membership formed an integral part of a broader 'flight' from institutional allegiance. As a result, individuals have came to rely less on absorbing a shared moral vision from established tradition and more on a privatised morality shaped by the forces operating in a pluralist and market society.

Gender roles and modern marriage

Family life is central to the reproduction of society. As a result, the characteristic patterns of relationship between men and women in marriage and the transmission of those patterns is inextricably linked to both the economic realities and the dominant cultural values and ethos of that society. At the heart of well-ordered post-war Britain lay a natural complementary 'givenness' in the roles and identity of men and women which focused on an economic division of labour between the 'breadwinning' husband and his 'homemaking' wife. This clear division of labour, alien to both a rural economy and our increasingly post-industrial world, had its roots in the development of Britain as an industrial society with its clear requirement for a separation of home and work. Nevertheless, it was asserted with renewed vigour in the 1950s, perhaps as part of an act of cultural amnesia designed to obviate the recent history of women running the country whilst their men folk were away at war. The enthusiasm for such a renewal can be amply illustrated from the content of women's magazines of the era, devoted as they were to talk of domesticity, the separate spheres of men and women, to respectability and religion. One clear example, comically remote to us, can be found in an edition of *Housekeeping Monthly* from 1951:

The Good Wife's Guide

Have dinner ready. Plan ahead, even the night before, to have a delicious meal ready for his return.

Prepare yourself. Touch up your make-up, put a ribbon in your hair and be fresh-looking.

Prepare the children. Take a few minutes to wash the children's hands and faces. They are little treasures and he would like to see them playing their part.

Listen to him. Let him talk first – remember his topics of conversation are more important than yours.

Don't complain if he's late for dinner or even if he stays out all night. Count this as minor compared to what he might have gone through that day.

A good wife always knows her place.[16]

Expanding horizons

The emergence of a new cultural world, which challenged such inherited wisdom and questioned the priority of the 'ribbon in your hair' (let alone not complaining if the man in your life is out all night), placed much greater emphasis on egalitarianism. More particularly, the growth of a feminist movement throughout the 1960s strongly committed to promoting 'equal rights' led, in combination with the expansion of education, to a shift in women's expectations of life. No longer was marriage and family the horizon of expectation for the upcoming generation of women. Following the implementation of the Robbins Report into Higher Education (1963), the numbers continuing in education after 18 expanded greatly. Between 1962 and 1980, the female student population trebled whilst the number of males doubled, so that by the end of the period women made up over 40 per cent of the student body.[17] Inevitably this had an impact upon female aspirations and employment and led to a reduction in the number of women inclined to marry in their late teens and early twenties.

The crucial change, however, occurred in the workplace with the removal of marriage as a bar to employment. Whereas around two-thirds of single women were economically active from the Edwardian period through to the present, marriage was perceived to be in direct conflict with employment outside the home. In the year of the advice to wives quoted above, less than one quarter of married women (22 per cent) were in any form of employment. However, by 1971 this had doubled (42 per cent) and by 1991, more than half of women (53 per cent) were employed outside the home.[18] In addition, a progressive widening of the range of employment opportunities for women, declining occupational segregation and, of course, the introduction of the Equal Pay Act of 1970 and the Sex Discrimination Act of 1975, led to a significant reduction in income differentials between the sexes.

As women experienced increasing autonomy and independence through their involvement with employment, there was a 'knock-on' effect for the marriage relationship. Success in the public world of work often liberated women from socially prescribed roles – they were no longer simply a 'wife and mother'. As a result, marriage came to be seen more as an individually negotiated partnership. Furthermore, it was a partnership more easily dissolved as the possibility of financial independence lowered the 'costs' of divorce for women.

Equality and its limits

Whilst the expansion of economic possibilities has been quite significant, it would be absurd to argue that traditional roles have been completely overturned and that our society is now gender-blind. Rather, gender remains a powerful factor influencing and shaping everyday life. The movement of women into the world of work does not, for example, seem to have been accompanied by a comparable movement of men into the home, at least in terms of contributions to house-work.[19] Indeed, as a consequence of having to balance paid employment, childcare and housework, '... the tension between family and work may have become more severe, more visible and more prevalent'[20] for the majority of modern women.

Yet the principle of equality is perceived by couples to be central to their relationship. In their study of newlyweds who had married in 1979, Mansfield and Collard found that couples interviewed six years later '... accepted that... modern marriage should be and was a partnership of equals', yet they also concurred that '... for circumstantial reasons their marriage could not be entirely equal.' For such couples equality was expressed in terms of a '... workable equity, based not so much on a *quid pro quo* as on fairness and balance.' Such an approach to equality which conceives of it in terms of mutual reciprocity involved 'the blending of a notion of equivalence with the concept of "being at one".' At root then, such equality was understood in terms of similarity, 'the identification with likeness', rather than being focused on an integration of two separate people. Yet behind this cosy picture of togetherness, Mansfield and Collard discern two different agendas. Her agenda is characterised in terms of the desire for 'a common life'; the sharing of interests and spending time together, especially talking. His desire is more for a 'life in common'; for the sharing of similar goals, yet the retention of some degree of separation. Characteristically, this latter male view of marriage incorporates more of the elements of traditional marriage.[21] Hence:

> ... the biggest difficulty for married couples is accepting the gulf between the modern notion of marriage as an experience of 'one-ness', and the reality of marriage as a

relationship requiring constant negotiations between two different people.[22]

Institution to relationship

The sheer speed of cultural change over the course of a generation or so has had a profound impact upon the man–woman relationship. One simple (and to a degree simplifying) way of capturing this shift in the meaning of marriage is in terms of a transition from an *institution*, formed and authorised by external factors like legislation, strength of custom and tradition or Church ritual, to *relationship*, authenticated internally by the couple themselves on the strength of mutual affection and regard. Obviously, there are elements of the institutional and relational in all marriages, but there is strong evidence to suggest a significant shift in emphasis over the last few decades, transforming it from a community of need premised upon an absolute commitment, a clear-cut division of labour between husband and wife and an emphasis on its public aspect into an ongoing 'do-it-yourself' project which privileges the emotional and interpersonal aspects of an essential private relationship between a couple.

This transition can be illustrated extensively from survey material which seeks to answer the question: 'What factors contribute to a successful marriage?' Here a shift can be charted from an emphasis on practical and economic factors (living apart from in-laws, adequate income, good housing) in the 1950s to one on personal and emotional factors (mutual respect and appreciation, understanding and tolerance, tastes and interests in common) by the 1990s. So, for example, in 1952, 70 per cent of British people interviewed highlighted an adequate income as an important factor, and 63 per cent good housing, in the making of a successful marriage, whereas by 1990, 34 per cent of people cited adequate income and 37 per cent good housing. Conversely, in 1952, 29 per cent cited

tastes and interests in common compared with 49 per cent in
1990.[23]

Naturally, such changes reflect changing economic realities,
but they also provide a clear indication of a shift in ideas
concerning the 'project' of marriage from stress on the successful completion of roles of homemaker and breadwinner
to a togetherness based on intimacy, with greater expectations
of partners as individuals as well as spouses. Nevertheless,
the basic economic functions are still integral to the success
of a marriage relationship, even if they are given less priority
by couples, with the result that, as the historian Gillis notes:

> People expect more of the conjugal relationship. It is
> made to bear the full weight of needs for intimacy, com-
> panionship, and love, needs which were previously met
> in other ways.[24]

Beyond the 'permissive society'

Above I have described the changes that have occurred within
family life over the last few decades as revolutionary. This is
not intended as hyperbole or rhetoric: there has been a profound shift in people's behaviour and in the social norms that
govern society. So far in this chapter we have considered
that revolution from the perspective of the individual in
relation to external authority and in terms of the transformation of the role of women within society. Now I wish to turn
and look at an even more profoundly changed relationship,
that between ourselves and our bodies, or more particularly
between our sexuality and the conception of children, and
the consequences of this transformation.

Prompted by the emphasis which Augustine places on an
openness to conception as a defining element of marriage, it
is the acceptance of family limitation and subsequently, with
advances in contraception, of family planning which I believe

involves the most radical break with the Christian past. The earliest, cautious endorsement for contraception from within the Christian fold came from a number of Nonconformist ministers at the very end of the nineteenth century, but it was not until the Lambeth Conference of 1930 that the Anglican Church, after much debate, accepted in principle the permissibility of contraception, under certain quite prescribed conditions. This initially quite grudging concession that couples might have recourse to physical methods of contraception 'to limit and avoid parenthood ... where there is a morally sound reason for avoiding complete abstinence'[25] was followed in 1958 by a more ringing endorsement, which might be regarded as representative of the contemporary Protestant Christian position:

> The Conference believes that the responsibility for deciding upon the number and frequency of children has been laid by God upon the conscience of parents everywhere; that this planning, in such ways as are mutually acceptable to husband and wife in Christian Conscience, is a right and important factor in Christian family life and should be the result of positive choice before God. Such responsible parenthood, built on obedience to all the duties of marriage, requires a wise stewardship of the resources and the abilities of the family as well as a thoughtful consideration of the varying population needs and problems of society and the claims of future generations.[26]

However, the advent of new contraceptive methods in the 1960s facilitated changing attitudes and practices and have subsequently resulted in the unravelling of the intimate connection between marriage, childbearing and sexuality. For the sociologist Peter Berger, the advent and acceptability of modern contraceptive methods has led in his judgement to a 'Promethean break' with the past.[27] Similarly, the eminent

Christian ethicist, Lady Helen Oppenheimer, argues that: ' . . . it is hard to overestimate the difference that reliable birth control has made.'[28] Whilst the churches have considered contraception as an ethical issue in principle, they have not paid sufficient attention to the full social and psychological implications that the ability to 'plan a family' has brought. This enhanced ability to control procreation has set in motion a chain of developments connecting the sexual, procreative and relationship formation behaviour of men and women over the second half of the twentieth century which is described by those social scientists whose concern is understanding population change under the banner of the 'second demographic transition'[29] or 'The Second Contraceptive Revolution'.[30] But to understand this evolution in social ecology more fully we need to turn back the clock a century.

A silent revolution

The modern world is founded upon a number of key structural transformations. One of the most obvious and far-reaching of these revolutionised the economy: the Industrial Revolution. Equally important, though we are perhaps less aware of it, has been a profound structural change in the human population, commonly known as the (first) demographic transition. That transition involved a shift from a world marked by high birth and high death rates (at least in the so-called developed countries) to one in which premature death is now uncommon and large families few and far between.

 Between 1860 and 1920 birth rates began to fall significantly in an historically unprecedented fashion – a profound and far-reaching change took place across the nations of Europe which would come to transform family life irrevocably. This transformation, the advent of family limitation on a population-wide scale, was, in Susan Watkins memorable phrase, achieved ' . . . with primitive technology and without generals.'[31] that is, with *coitus interruptus* and in the face of opposition from Church, State and often, the medical establishment.

Whilst methods for preventing contraception have been known to human cultures for centuries, even millennia, the shift in family size that took place during this period was not the result of contraceptive innovation, but rather of changed hearts and minds. Limiting family size became an acceptable moral option; it was no longer 'unthinkable'. A silent revolution in practical morality conducted by ordinary people in the privacy of their own homes had taken place.

For demographers, this innovation possessed a certain intrinsic logic. Mortality rates had fallen considerably across north-western Europe in the nineteenth century, a process that accelerated from 1850 when the life expectancy of the under-fives improved dramatically. As a result, the population in the United Kingdom increased from 16 to 42 million between 1800 and 1900 and for both economic and cultural reasons there existed a strong imperative for couples to have smaller families. For a culture whose primary understanding of marriage was that it was 'ordained for the increase of mankind according to the will of God'[32] this development was of the utmost significance. Whilst couples in this period and well into the early twentieth century were engaged in 'stopping' behaviour, that is they practised family limitation rather than family planning, this popular and pragmatic innovation laid the foundations for a sequence of events which would later reconfigure the marriage relationship more dramatically.

In Western Europe, the age at which people have married and therefore started a family has over the centuries always been closely related to the achievement of economic independence. The combination of growing affluence and the acceptance of family limitation led throughout the first half of the twentieth century to a gradual downward shift in the age at which people married and an increase in the proportion in each generation who married. This trend reached its height in the wake of post-war prosperity in the late fifties and early sixties, the 'golden age' of marriage had arrived: marriage, sex and childbearing had rarely been so tightly bound together.

The 'Promethean break' and its consequences

As we have suggested above however, all this changed rapidly over the next decade or so and the advent of new contraceptive methods played a clear catalytic role. The task of simply limiting the number of births within a family had been achieved in the first few decades of the twentieth century – what the new contraceptive methods brought, through their effectiveness, was a much greater degree of control. Characteristically, those marrying in the 1950s, like their parents, only married when they were ready for parenthood: marriage and starting a family was seen as 'the same thing'. For them contraception, however achieved, was an exercise in limitation; it was for 'stopping'. What the new contraceptive innovations brought, through their effectiveness, was a much higher degree of flexibility and thus a much greater range of possible goals; the Pill or IUD could be used within marriage to delay a first birth or to plan and space children, in addition to preventing pre-nuptial pregnancy or births outside marriage.

The initial impact of the Pill and the IUD upon marital sexuality in the early 1960s was a subtle one. In a world in which pre-marital sex was still counter to prevailing mores, it permitted people to marry even younger without that being a commitment to starting a family – an attractive possibility in a world with increasing educational and economic possibilities for young women. The first subtle intimations of change were, therefore, an increase in subsequent years for newlyweds of the gap between marriage and first birth – a crucial step weakening the link between marriage and reproduction. For the first time ever in Britain, marriage ceased to be the automatic threshold for fertility. Choice and conscious planning were thus entering into an area hitherto the domain of the 'taken for granted', the assumed. Couples increasingly began to face a new decision: when to interrupt contraceptive practice in order to conceive.

Whilst it is notoriously difficult to measure, there is a reasonable amount of evidence to suggest that a greater proportion of couples engaged in pre-marital sexual experience after the Second World War than before. Such change was perhaps inevitable given the extensive disruptions to ordered civilian life that living through war produced and, indeed, the widespread availability of condoms to the forces. Pre-marital sexual activity increased significantly in the 1950s and this trend continued throughout the 1960s.[33] As modern contraception spread to the unmarried population (the Pill was available to unmarried women from 1971) the number of women pregnant at the altar, however perceptibly, began to fall, 'shotgun' marriages virtually disappeared and the age of first marriage began to rise. Pre-marital sexual experience, frowned upon in the 1950s had became acceptable twenty years later. Even with a continuing 'double standard', only one in four brides in the early 1970s claimed no experience prior to marriage.[34]

The extent of this change can be briefly illustrated through a consideration of the 'biography' of the statistically 'average' woman as she experiences these important transitions in her personal life. In the early 1960s our 'everywoman' typically began her first sexual relationship on marriage at the age of 23, with her first baby being born a year later. By the early 1970s, she had become sexually active in her late teens, married a little later at 24 and bore her first child two years later. Today, she is likely to be sexually active at 16, the legal age of consent, marrying well over a decade later at 28 after a period of two or three years in a cohabiting relationship with her partner. If she has not already given birth before tying the knot, then she is likely to have her first child at 30. From this brief sketch of a 'normal biography' as it has evolved over the period, we can see how profound the changes have been. There is, however, a significant caveat to add: an increasing proportion of women in each decade have experienced relationship breakdown, diluting the sense in which one can speak of a 'normal biography' at all.

The emergence of cohabitation

With increasing numbers of young men and women leaving home and living independently in their early twenties and with near-universal pre-marital sexual experience premised on a clear separation of sexuality from procreation, widespread but discreet 'sleeping together' evolved rapidly into the more public and acknowledged practice of 'living together'. The speed of this social transformation is noteworthy: cohabitation in the late 1960s and early 1970s had been the unconventional choice of an unconventional minority, with around one in twenty of those marrying having lived together first, yet by the late 1980s those marrying directly had become the minority. The latest reliable figure suggests that 77 per cent of couples had cohabited beforehand.[35] Furthermore the proportion of all couples within the population in a cohabiting relationship (rather than married) tripled between 1986 and 1999 from 5 per cent to 15 per cent.[36]

The diffusion of 'living together'

One way to understand this rapid transformation of cohabitation, from the stigmatised behaviour of a minority to a widespread and conventional life-stage choice is through the idea
of the 'mental cohort'. Each generation of people passing
through the various stages makes decision which then both
constrain and enrich the options for the next group. As a
result, each successive peer group considering their attitudes
to sex, relationships and becoming a parent is aware of the
acceptability of the different choices open to them as a
member of a particular social grouping in society, whether
that group be 'deviant', unconventional, fairly normal or conservative. Thus the spectrum of acceptable behaviour
'available' to the university-educated children of the Home
Counties 'gin and jag' belt will be quite different to the young
people brought up on inner-city housing estates or indeed
those from more isolated and traditional rural communities.
Indeed, ' . . . it is through the choice that people make with
regard to such life shaping demographic events as marriage,
having a child, and method of contraception, that people
express their sense of belonging to a certain sub-group.'[37]

Innovative behaviour then spreads from those groups with
less conventional and more 'progressive' views, generally the
young, educated, urban-dwelling and less religious to the rest
of society. One consequence of this is that at various points of
the transition, the 'behaviour' in question, will 'look and
feel' different. This is clearly the case with cohabitation: the
earliest innovators cohabited characteristically out of an ideological opposition to marriage, whereas the majority of later
cohabitees may be more inclined to see living together as an
essential preparation for the desired state of marriage. One
result of this evolving situation is that pre-marital cohabitation is then associated with a higher relative risk of divorce

than marrying directly when it is a minority practice, and a lower rate of divorce once it has become a majority practice.

This is exactly what the evidence suggests. The first studies of cohabitation in Britain, which looked at those who cohabited in the early eighties, concluded that those who cohabit before marriage were 50 per cent more likely than those who married directly to be divorced within five years. This finding challenged the naïve proponents of 'trial marriage', who had assumed that cohabitation would have a beneficial effect on relationship stability, and confirmed the views of many Christians who argued that lack of commitment made living together inherently unstable. However, subsequent work by the same researcher based on data from the early 1990s undermined this confirmed viewpoint, for it found no difference in marital stability between those who married directly and those who had cohabited beforehand.[38]

Unsurprisingly, in addition to a change in behaviour, there has been a profound change of attitude. Cohabitation is not just tolerated, rather an increasing proportion of people now regard it as foolhardy not to cohabit. So, for example, the *British Social Attitudes* survey of 2000 asked 'is it a good idea for a couple who intend to get married to live together first?' Fifty-six per cent of British people interviewed believed that it was. [39]

Marriage and children

Whilst there are adults in cohabiting relationships of all ages, cohabitation is most common amongst those in their late twenties for whom it tends to be an experience of brief duration, on average three years, before ending either in separation or more commonly for those entering their first union, in marriage. For many, the decision to cohabit marks the transition to adult independence, and a period of living together has therefore become a life-stage blurring the traditional boundary between courtship and the early stages of marriage.[40] If we accept that cohabitation does 'blur' these two previously separate stages of courtship and marriage, then the fact that a significant number of cohabiting relationships do end in separation after a short period should not in itself come as a surprise to us – courtship is by definition a process, the breakdown of it, an ever-present reality.

Nevertheless, the majority of cohabitees do in fact express a strong intention to marry at some point in the future. That intention is most commonly related to one of two motivations – a desire to confirm or 'flag up' a couple's commitment to lifelong union or because a couple have decided that they wish to have children together within formal marriage.[41]

One of the hallmarks of contemporary Western society is the postponement of, or even flight from, parenthood. This can be seen in countries with high rates of cohabitation like Sweden or Norway, but also in nations where cohabitation is relatively uncommon. Indeed Catholic Italy has one of the lowest birth rates in the world.[42] The birth of a child is a highly significant psychological juncture in the modern relationship which often brings financial and emotional challenges to a dual-earning companionate model of marriage. Sadly, it is also a well-documented trigger point for the beginnings of relationship disillusionment and breakdown.[43] Parenthood is not, then, a venture upon which prudent modern couples embark too quickly. In this context, the desire for cohabiting couples to marry on contemplating the prospect of parenthood makes sound sense: it echoes the clear historic connection which underlies the traditional cultural understanding of marriage, and the arrival of dependants is also the point at which the State takes a more active interest in supporting marriage. Indeed, it asserts that 'marriage is still the surest foundation for raising children.'[44]

This last assertion is in fact strongly supported by the evidence, for whilst it is clear that marital stability *per se* is not effected by premarital cohabitation,[45] children born to cohabiting parents are twice as likely to experience parental separation as those born within marriage.[46] In re-evaluating cohabitation as an integral part of the process by which people become married, an authentically Christian assessment should tie parenthood to a public, explicit and legal commitment.

A panoramic approach

It is often assumed that marriage and cohabitation are alternatives, that they are 'market competitors', representing mutually exclusive pathways or responses to a world devoid of the 'signposts established by tradition'. A clear example of this approach can be found in Patricia Morgan's book *Marriage Lite*.[47] Here marriage and cohabitation are presented as 'essentially different', as polar opposites, and a whole wealth of data is deployed to suggest that marriage is associated with responsible family behaviour, whereas cohabitation encourages inadequate and even anti-social behaviour. Indeed, the presentation is almost biblical in its resonance, conjuring the Old Testament teaching of Proverbs with its 'two paths', that of wisdom and responsibility and that of folly and godlessness.

Such a polarisation, however superficially attractive it may seem to some, is not however justified by the evidence. Rather, it makes a good deal more sense to consider contemporary marriage and cohabitation in relation to each other. One obvious reason for doing so is that three-quarters of those who marry cohabit beforehand, and, as has been suggested, such an experience of 'living together' is increasingly part of the 'normal' transition to marriage. Clearly there are *some* cohabiting relationships that lack an interest in, or commitment to, building a common life in a permanent, exclusive and publicly recognised relationship. Such relationships might rightly be regarded as *non-nuptial*. However, we need to be careful here, for such a description could equally be applied to those couples who, whilst not formally married, live out a relationship in the 'Christian spirit' embodying what Augustine called the 'goods' of marriage within their union – children, fidelity and the mutual concord that lies at the heart of the idea of sacrament. Many cohabiting relationships, indeed I would suggest the majority, are explicitly or implicitly *pre-nuptial*.[48] That is, the couple in question see their relationship as a prelude to and sometimes a preparation for formal marriage in the not-too-distant future.

A second reason for challenging the sharp distinction often drawn between marriage and cohabitation is that the 'institution' of marriage is not 'what it used be'. A generation ago, social scientists would consider the 'problem of divorce' and hunt for factors that predisposed individuals to marital breakdown,[49] based on the assumption that such dissolution of relationships was exceptional and a 'pathological' event which could be explained on a medical model of health and dis-ease. However, the evolution of a mass-divorce society has refocused the debate – explanation is no longer sought at the level of the individual, rather the diagnosis lies deeper with marriage itself. The radical changes outlined in the previous chapter – the separation of sexuality from procreation, the increased emphasis on equality between the sexes, and above all the broad shift that we have characterised as one from 'institution' to 'relationship' – have rendered the project of the lifelong union between a man and a woman a 'problematic' venture.

As our opening quotation from Saint Augustine suggests, to draw a clear-cut distinction between unions based on whether a couple have undergone a formal ceremony or not is to miss the point. What lies at the heart of the marriage relationship is what the ceremony exists to bear witness to, namely intention and commitment. As the influential sociologist of the family, Jessie Barnard pointed out thirty years ago:

> One fundamental fact underlies the conception of marriage itself. Some kind of commitment must be involved. Without such commitment a marriage may hardly be said to exist at all . . . The form of the commitment is less important than the emotional contents it underlies. It may be a written contract or simply vows and promises made before witnesses *or even simply an 'understanding' or consensual arrangement.* (my emphasis)[50]

For those with an active interest in the state of the man–woman relationship in our society today, a panoramic approach must therefore be taken, which looks beyond the categories of marriage and cohabitation to interpret the character of intimacy, sexuality, identity and particularly the nature of commitment, both its establishment within cohabitation and its maintenance within marriage. In short, we must 'unpack' the reality behind the *relationship*, for as the eminent sociologist, Zygmunt Bauman puts it, relationships are 'the sole game in town worth playing.'[51]

CHAPTER FIVE

Love in a chaotic climate

In the preceding chapter we argued that over the last few decades men and women have been caught up in the throes of a relationship revolution so far-reaching as to bear comparison with the shift in economic regimes between feudalism and capitalism. This revolution has been characterised by an unprecedented emphasis on the individual who navigates his or her way through life without the aid of the clear signposts provided by tradition or custom. In addition, contraceptive innovation has transformed the human inscape, reconfiguring the relationship between self and sexuality. If this analysis is broadly correct, then we should think of the rapid escalation in cohabitation as more of a symptom than an agent of social change.

Revolutions by their nature generate a great deal of turbulence and are difficult to comprehend from within. Therefore, Christians seeking to discern an approach to contemporary marriage and cohabitation would be wise to pay attention to the descriptions and interpretations offered by social scientists. In this chapter, therefore, we shall consider two contrasting and influential approaches to understanding and mapping the confusing terrain that is modern loving: that of Anthony Giddens with his advocacy of what he calls the 'pure relationship' and that of Beck and Beck-Gernsheim who argue that in a post-modern world fraught with uncertainty, the pursuit of romantic love is increasing coming to resemble a 'secular religion'.

The 'Pure Relationship'

Perhaps the most influential attempt to map this evolving landscape is that of the prominent sociologist – Anthony Giddens (he of the 'Third Way'). In *The Transformation of Intimacy*[1] he argues that the changes outlined in our previous chapter, in particular the separation of sexuality from procreation, have given birth to a new social institution: marriage and the ideal of romantic love have, in this view been displaced as *the* frame of reference for intimacy between men and women. Rather, Giddens argues, a new 'institution' is emerging which is increasingly redefining the nature of the man–woman relationship. This new phenomenon he labels: the 'pure relationship'.

Such a relationship is 'pure' in the sense of being unfettered by convention, role or social rules. It is entered into ' . . . for what can be derived by each person from a sustained association with another.' Furthermore, 'it is continued only in so far as it is thought by both parties to deliver enough satisfactions for each individual to stay within it.'[2] Whether people cohabit or are formally married, so Giddens argues, the relationship between heterosexual (and also homosexual) love and sexuality is defined by this new way of 'relating', constituted by a different sort of love which he labels 'confluent love'. Confluent loving is an active but a contingent form of love. It is not necessarily monogamous: sexual exclusiveness only 'has a role in the relationship to the degree to which the partners mutually deem it desirable or essential', nor indeed is there any commitment to permanence. Rather what keeps a couple together 'is the acceptance on the part of each partner, "until further notice", that each gains sufficient benefit from the relation to make its continuance worthwhile.'[3]

This new way of loving clearly ' . . . jars with the "for-ever", "one-and-only" qualities'[4] central to our ideas of romantic love. But for Giddens this jarring is a good thing, for in his analysis romantic love with its desire to become 'one' with the beloved is the product of a patriarchal society; it is intimately associated with (and therefore tainted by) inequality between the sexes. In such a view, romantic love is rooted in a clear complementarity between the sexes that functions to 'mask' the oppression of woman. Thus the breadwinner/homemaker marriage of the Fifties provides Giddens with a clear example: the high cultural value placed upon the adored wife and mother in the home is unmasked as a strategy to keep women in thrall to the service and servicing of 'their man'.

Female sexual emancipation and autonomy is therefore in direct conflict with the ideal of romantic love and Giddens' replacement for it – *confluent love* – is therefore envisaged by the sociologist as the '... medium of a wide-ranging emotional reorganisation of social life.'[5] So, he argues, the 'pure relationship' has, courtesy of the contraceptive revolution described above, brought in its wake, a '... final liberation for sexuality, which thence can become wholly a quality of individuals and their transactions with one another.'[6] Having previously been tied through its procreative function to strong, even coercive, social norms and customs, sexuality has now been set free. It has become a 'property' which the individual can deploy as he or she sees fit; it has attained a certain lightness, or in Giddens' conception – '*plasticity*'. Thus, Giddens finds some merits in what the rest of us might call 'one-night stands':

> ... even in the shape of impersonal, fleeting contacts, episodic sexuality may be a positive form of everyday experiment. It reveals plastic sexuality for what it (implicitly) is: sex detached from its age-old subservience to differential power.[7]

A democratic love

At the heart of this transformation of intimacy that Giddens seeks to describe is 'the radical democratisation of the personal.'[8] Intimate relationships are thus the final frontier for the democratic impulse. This is what drives the current turmoil of the relationship revolution, the establishment of 'free and equal relations between individuals'. In this essentially political process, the consciousness raising and mobilisation is effected by a new form of pamphleteering, which flows from a therapeutic industry composed of self-help manuals, columnists and other 'experts' (or as often sexperts), there to assist with the liberation of individuals, that they might find their true selves. As with all enfranchising processes, autonomy is key:

> The principle of autonomy provides the guiding thread and the most important substantive component of these processes. In the arena of personal life, autonomy means the successful realisation of ... self – the condition of relating to others in an egalitarian way.[9]

For advocates of the 'pure relationship' and kindred concepts, like that of 'sexual citizenship',[10] the new world that is coming into existence is one in which the 'language of obligation and duty', characteristic of an imposed traditional morality informed by Christian belief is displaced by the practices of 'negotiated commitment and mutual responsibility,'[11] to be achieved by autonomous individuals.

Persons and consumers

The 'pure relationship' is intended by Giddens to be a reasonably accurate sociological description of 'where we are', but also a prescriptive account, an achievable, desirable new place that couples might increasingly come to inhabit. These two elements are difficult to separate. In places, Giddens paints an almost utopian vision, for example in the assertion that the pure relationship could bring about 'the reconciliation of the sexes'.[12] Whilst the proposal does incorporate a number of attractive features, especially through its unflinching commitment to a real equality of the sexes, there are difficulties with the account, both as an accurate description of the status quo, and as a vision for human flourishing. This centres on his account of personhood and his assumption that the rules which operate in the public domain can simply be transferred to the sphere of personal relationships.

The most striking aspect of Giddens' vision for a new intimacy is the way in which he transfers notions of rationality that operate in the public domain into the private sphere. 'Pure' relationships are entered into, and sustained (for as long as they are maintained) only in so far as they meet the needs, desires or current 'life projects' of the individual concerned. In such an account, the sexual and emotional dimensions of a relationship are seen as subservient to a cost–benefit calculation. The individual is conceived to be, in the heart of their identity, not a citizen, let alone a whole person, but, I would suggest, a *consumer*: an autonomous rational and free agent engaging in a market with other such beings on a clearly contractual basis. Such a reductive and cynical understanding is clearly a hopelessly impoverished and inadequate account of the human person, for it precludes the possibility for real human encounter and the growth of trust that lies at the heart of a relationship and which is based upon mutual vulnerability.

There is no doubt that the concept of the 'pure relationship' contains more than a grain of truth, for it 'highlights real tendencies in how many contemporary persons are inclined to understand their sexual relationships.'[13] One clear example of this understanding taking shape can be found in the emergence of a lifestyle practised by a small number of urban couples labelled 'living-apart-together', in which sexually intimate couples reject the 'interdependency associated with love on a daily basis' by maintaining separate households and high levels of independence.[14] Yet, given that we live in a fast-moving consumerist culture which places a great stress upon the individual, it would be extraordinary if our personal lives were not to some degree infected by utilitarian calculation. This doesn't mean however that it is the characteristic that defines contemporary relationships. Furthermore, it would be sociologically naïve to think that people's own rationalisations of their behaviour and their self-understandings of their actions constitute the lived reality. Similarly, it would be curious if the value ascribed by Giddens to autonomy and independence went unchallenged. The description of the pure relationship is then, I would suggest, too one-dimensional, too 'thin': it needs fleshing out with other elements.

The reality of risk

One central element that is missing from Giddens' account concerns the issue of risk. Risk and its calculation are central to the relationship game. One clear illustration of the role that calculating risk plays can be seen from the fact that a disproportionate number of the young people who entered cohabiting relationships rather than marrying directly in the early 1980s were those who had experienced parental divorce. Having witnessed marital failure at first hand, they themselves are more inclined to be cautious in their commitment. Unsurprisingly, an appreciation of the risks associated with traditional marriage is very much to the fore in Giddens' account of the transformation of intimacy. Marriage, with its progressive interdependence and entanglement in inherited gender roles, is perceived to enmesh individuals in a 'commitment trap'. This is especially the case for women: the two become one person, and that one person is the husband. Thus runs a commonplace feminist critique of marriage, grounded in what was for a long time the legal reality, and it is to avoid such a possibility, that many avoid the 'old way' of marriage. Yet it would be a touch naïve to think that stifling commitment was the only trap available to contemporary individuals, or indeed that the 'pure relationship' was devoid of risk. Far from it: Giddens' description of the 'pure relationship' as one 'until further notice' skates swiftly over an unsettling and troublesome reality. For the key satisfactions to be derived from a relationship – comfort, support, the sharing of hopes and dreams – cannot be divorced from the idea of security. Emotional security is, however, exactly what the pure relationship can never deliver, for being in such a relationship requires constant vigilance and the daily dread that notice could be given. Thus, whilst rescued from the trap of commitment inherent in marriage, individuals are subsequently condemned to an anxiety-laden freedom. As Zygmunt Bauman points out:

> By all accounts, relationship seen as a business transaction is not a cure for insomnia ... Loneliness spawns insecurity – but relationship seems to do nothing else. In a relationship, you may feel as insecure as without it, or worse. Only the names you give your anxiety change.

Furthermore,

> Once insecurity creeps in, navigation is never confident, thoughtful and steady. Rudderless, the frail raft of relationship sways between one and the other of the two ill-famed rocks on which many a partnership flounders: total submission and total power, meek acceptance and arrogant conquest, effacing one's own autonomy and stifling the autonomy of the partner.[15]

The challenge of chemistry

However, the most central omission from Giddens' rather clinical account comes under the broad heading of 'chemistry'. Before they can be maintained or regulated, relationships need to be initiated, and it is very difficult to see how a pure relationship can 'get off the ground': Giddens' 'economic' model of the individual takes no account of what we might describe as the pre-contractual foundations of relationships, the chemistry that draws them together. Even *if* partners to a 'pure' relationship were left unsullied by the whole emotional repertoire that occurs when a couple 'fall in love', the initiation of their relationship cannot be reduced to a purely rational process. Becoming an 'item' involves some degree of idealisation of the other and some desire to merge together, to become one, and such a process of merging is essential for achieving a sense of belonging and for providing a framework for the initial development of trust in the other. However rational and autonomous individuals may strive to be in their agency, relationships are founded through a dissolution of individuality to form a new 'society of two'. It is such emotional (and physiological) chemistry, rather than rational will, that underlies relationships and generates a personal and social bond, a 'conjugal' structure.

One of the key ideological dividing lines in Western society since the 1960s has been between two views of sexuality – the libertarian or hedonistic and what might be called the romantic. In the former view, sexuality is a positive, beneficial, joyous phenomenon. It is closely connected to self-fulfilment, personal health, happiness and indeed social progress. Whilst it may involve acts of affection, love or procreation, it is primarily a medium of pleasure, an expression of the self. The latter 'romantic' view, held by Christians (among others) sees sexuality not as an end in itself, but as a medium of love. Here sexuality is person-centred and looks to an expression that is tender, caring, loving and respectful. It is worth calling to mind from Chapter 2 one of the clearest articulations of this viewpoint from the document: *Marriage and the Church's Task*. Here sexual union:

> ... is not to be comprehended simply in terms of two individuals' experience of ecstatic pleasure. Such it certainly may be, but it is always more. It is an act of personal commitment that spans past, present and future. It is a celebration, healing, renewed pledge and promise. Sexual intercourse can 'mean' many different things to husband and wife, according to mood and circumstance. Above all, it communicates the affirmation of mutual belonging.[16]

As the ethicist Helen Oppenheimer puts it, what is problematic therefore with sexual expression outside the committed relationship is 'not that something unauthorized is being done ... but on the contrary that something deeply belonging to our human nature is *lacking*.'[17]

It is on account of this lack that the romantic fears the possibility of sexual objectification, dehumanisation and the promotion of relational instability. In contemporary society these two views are both commonly held: it is indisputable that sex is widely perceived as an autonomous sphere of pleasure, a body-oriented site for hedonistic self-expression on the part of the individual. Furthermore, in line with Giddens' emphasis on the individual consumer, sexuality is, through identification with the idea of 'lifestyle' becoming a commercial enterprise, forming part of the leisure, and even the fashion 'industry'. This is especially clear with the recent expansion of an erotica market produced by women for women: TV programmes like *Sex in the City* and *Sex Tips for Girls* have promoted a culture in which erotica is linked with female empowerment (e.g. Internet pornography, swinging parties, new 'girl only' sex clubs like 'Cake' in New

York). It is perhaps a sign of the times that a generation on from Anita Roddick who founded the Body Shop and made people feel good about pampering their bodies, her daughter Sam is behind the new erotica emporium 'Coco de Mer' based in Covent Garden.[18]

Anthony Giddens makes the claim that 'confluent love develops as an ideal in a society where almost everyone has the chance to become sexually accomplished.'[19] The romantic remains sceptical about the nature of such accomplishment, suspecting in the words of one sexologist that: 'everyone is in the know, and no one has the faintest idea.'[20] The vision of sexuality propounded by hedonistic individualism is in fact in opposition to that which is genuinely erotic. In reducing the purpose of sexuality to pleasure, it has become as one-dimensional as earlier Stoic accounts limiting sexuality to procreation. Sexuality is no longer mystified and enchanted, rather it is part of the realm of sober calculation and the power of reductive knowledge. A stark illustration of this comes from the writing of the French novelist Michel Houellebecq in his bleak portrayal of our atomised society in which religion has been replaced by trivial New Age philosophies and love has given way to meaningless sexual encounter:

> "Thanks" she said. Then she got up, put on her sweatshirt and filled their glasses up again.
>
> "It was really good in the jacuzzi just now . . ." said Bruno " . . . I still hadn't really seen your face. There was something pure about it – no seduction."
>
> "It all depends on Krause's corpuscles," Christiane said smiling . . . "The shaft of the clitoris and the glans of the penis are covered in Krause's corpuscles, rich in nerve endings. When touched, they cause a powerful flow of endorphins in the brain. The penis and the clitoris have

about the same number ... – sexual equality goes that far."[21]

In its insistence on placing rational calculation rather than emotional bonding at the centre of its account of sexuality, the 'pure relationship' denies a role to self-transcendence. Rather then entailing a sexual liberation, there is, in fact no place left for the genuinely erotic:

> Pure relationships are clearly unable to cope with sweaty, heaving and breathless bodies, animalistic urges and sexual fluids which might colonize the mind and interfere, however temporarily, with the reflexive and democratic processes of 'talk work' central to 'confluent love'.[22]

... and of children

The final exclusion from Giddens' purified vision of human relationships should now be obvious: the world of the pure relationship is one inhabited by adults only. Children simply do not figure where intimacy has been so transformed. This is not entirely surprisingly given that human desire is framed in terms of contract and personal development. For, why, given effective contraception and the availability of abortion, when child-free relationships are a distinct possibility, would one bother to have children? One answer might be to envisage children as a form of consumer durable, objects of 'emotional consumption' within the 'pure relationship'. Yet children pose a highly conspicuous threat of pollution to such purity – sullying adult independence and autonomy in myriad ways. Thus the fact that dependent beings demanding unconditional love and self-sacrifice are omitted from this Giddens' account is of no real surprise. Having children is an open-ended commitment rather than a transient project: their nurture requires love, tenderness and stability. Such needs can hardly be met by the fluidity of a 'til further notice' relationship.

The persistence and the paradox of modern love

At the heart of Anthony Giddens' attempt to interpret the transformations that have occurred within the man–woman relationship in the last few decades lies an assumption that what applies in the public domain will ultimately come to apply to the private world. And indeed there is no doubt that rational processes have been, and will continue to be, appropriated to the sphere of personal life. One clear example of this is in the arena of mate selection. Here it is quite clear that the 'signposts', established by the customs and practices of traditional courtship, are now completely blank. Men and women can no longer rely on well-established same-sex peer groups or their membership of social groups with clearly defined social status to determine, at least in part, the suitability of a potential partner. For there has been a complete breakdown of these older traditions, customs and guidelines governing courtship and the selection of a suitable partner. Ironically, the clearest indication of this is the success in the USA of *The Rules*, a guide to dating and courting for 90's women that promises a 'Mr Right for the new millennium' as long as they adopt 'The Rules', a dating strategy based on courtship etiquette from the 1950s.[23]

This lack of guidelines has greatly increased the complexity involved in discerning the suitability of a potential mate at a time when our emotional demands of a relationship have soared. Given the high valuation ascribed to the virtue of efficiency in our technocratic society, it is perhaps unsurprising that a huge increase in standardised screening criteria has evolved to allow people the possibility of screening out potentially undesirable mates and therefore minimising the vulnerability of personal disclosure that modern 'courtship' demands. So, for example, as the space given over to personal advertising has expanded, the acronyms have proliferated, restricting in ever more specific and reductive ways what is acceptable to the individual in a language that the readership will understand. Thus SWPM, n/s 6'1" 42, ISO slim petite SBF n/s, 25–35 for LTR (single white professional male, non-smoker; in search of: single black female, non-smoker, for long-term relationship) is likely to come from the *Washington Post*, as equivalent adverts in the UK national press would be less likely to code ethnicity and would tend to include gsoh, or for readers of *Private Eye*, vgsoh. Thus are Cupid's arrows given so clear a direction. Time, like space, is also at a premium and so now, in the pursuit of efficiency, we have 'speed dating'. And at the end of all this, for the successful, the 'perfect' wedding day can then be packaged and customised – like the modern computer with its bundle of software – with a 'top of the range' honeymoon.

There is little doubt then that consumer-like decision-making has made extensive cut-ways for its highway through the domain of the personal. Yet, 'curiouser and curiouser', if relationships are so contractually pure, why should the 'perfect' wedding day matter? This is one of the paradoxes of contemporary marriage – despite widespread cohabitation, big 'white weddings' have not diminished. Indeed, they have increased: every couple, it seems, wants their day. For the social historian, John Gillis, rather than bystanders at the demise of romantic love, contemporary men and women have a greater need than ever to express their 'faith' in love, and the wedding is par excellence the vehicle for such expression:

> It seems that we are relying more and more on big weddings to sustain our faith in love. The fact that it no longer matters that the bride is pregnant, that the pair coming down the aisle is gay or lesbian, or that the couple

are both on their third or fourth marriages, is indicative of just how much the perfect couple still matters in Western culture'.[24]

So, we have the paradox of a highly commercial and extensive wedding industry facilitating a ritual that is intended to be the most intimate and fulfilling of personal experiences for the couple. Rather than heralding the demise of romantic love, it appears that a paradox lies at the heart of the modern pursuit of love: hand in hand with the relentless rise of autonomous individuals, calculators in hand, those same individuals experience an increasingly desperate need to escape, to move beyond the rationalising processes of contemporary living and create a 'society of two'.

The 'society of two'

There appears, then, to be a good deal more complexity to the terrain of contemporary relationships than is permitted by Giddens' view of the world. This brings us to a second interpretation of that terrain, the landscape of modern loving, that of German sociologists, Ulrich Beck and Elizabeth Beck-Gernsheim. In common with most contemporary sociologists, including Giddens, they place a great deal of emphasis on the importance of the shift from traditional authority to the individual: 'With a mysterious force, which they do not understand themselves, although they may personify it . . . people are shaking off rigid gender roles, bourgeois maxims, set ways.'[25] Furthermore, they too stress the intimate connections between the 'public' world (e.g. of employment) and the private world of the family. Beck-Gernsheim, in particular, draws attention to the striking similarities between changes in the family and the new 'topography of work'[26]. For as the post-war period has unfolded, a time of considerable stability with long-term, full-time employment protected by labour legislation has given way to the more varied and unstable working patterns marked by deregulation and flexibility with which we are so familiar. Greater mobility, fragility and uncertainty has, then, eroded the 'given' and fixed forms of operating in the different rooms that make up society. As the previously trusted walls have crumbled away, life has become a 'building-site'.[27] In this mapping of our post-modern world, employment and relationships are of a piece with the rest of social life: 'the family is *only the setting, not the cause* of events.'[28]

Where Beck and Beck-Gernsheim part company with Anthony Giddens is in their belief that humans have a basic need for a primary relationship, which gives them a sense of 'who I am'. In the contemporary world with its overwhelming emphasis on individual autonomy, the importance of personal relationships as an alternative 'place' from the public domain has been elevated: our 'private' lives are therefore experienced as 'more real' than our life in the public arena. With the relentless spread of *Homo economicus*, men and women long all the more for close, personal, emotional, intimate ties. The result is that there is an enhanced preoccupation with love relationships and an elaboration of the ideals associated with romantic love – spontaneity, emotional intensity and permanence. Far from romantic love being in decline, so Beck and Beck-Gernsheim argue, it ' . . . seems to promise a chance of being authentic in a world which otherwise runs on pragmatic solutions and convenient lies.'[29]

Contradictions

Yet there is an unfortunate Catch 22 here. The dilution of tradition sets up a dual dynamic. It frees men and women from traditional norms and expectations such that increasingly they see themselves as individuals, as 'Mark' or 'Sarah' over and against being 'a man' or 'a woman', but it also increases the attractions of and need for a close relationship with a unique other as *the* place of emotional fulfilment and identity formation in the context of weakened family and community ties. As a result, the stakes are raised in the 'relationship game', increasing the risk involved in making even a provisional commitment to another and raising the personal costs entailed in maintaining a relationship. Furthermore, the increased focus on the choice of the individual means that people assume more responsibility if their relationship flounders. In the past when there were 'scripts' for a 'good marriage' and clear expectations about what constituted a 'suitable match', a 'considerate' husband or 'dutiful' wife, external circumstances or parents could share the blame for failure, but with the enhanced role of personal choice, responsibility falls much more squarely upon the shoulders of the individual.

As we established in Chapter 4, people now expect their 'other halfs' to be everything to them: best friends and adventurous sexual partners, good economic providers and stimulating intellectual companions. Clearly, when the stakes are raised in such a fashion, the cracks will emerge, not least along the fractures of cultural contradiction. One such fracture lies with the great cultural emphasis placed upon the romantic in relationships, upon spontaneity and sexual performance, in the context of an everyday partnership which requires hard work and commitment, for by and large, 'Great lovers do not make for good housekeeping.'[30]

Another clear line of cultural contradiction concerns gender equality. Whilst a couple may hold and practise a relatively uncomplicated notion of equality prior to parenthood, becoming a mother and becoming a father are typically quite different social transitions, often bringing unexpected psychological 'baggage', unanticipated cultural expectations, and of course potentially, significant financial pressure. In becoming parents, 'Mark' and 'Sarah' discover very clearly that they are a 'man' and a 'woman' and forces beyond their control begin to prompt them down differentiated pathways, with children and the issues of economic dependence and interdependence playing a central role.

One way of understanding this divergence of the sexes is through a lament over the 'stalled' gender revolution: contraception, ease of divorce, increased educational and training opportunities and legislation, whilst leading to a significant increase in female engagement with the world of employment, has not resulted in the complete economic independence required for parity with men in terms of earnings and status at work. Indeed, many studies indicate that many women are disproportionately caught in a triple bind of paid employment, housework and childcare, whilst men's behaviour has not evolved to match the changes in female activity (see earlier note). This is a fairly accurate portrayal, yet it cannot be separated from a deeply held cultural view that children 'belong' with mothers rather than fathers, as witnessed by the majority of post-divorce arrangements. As Beck and Beck-Gernsheim point out:

> As long as women not only bear children but care for them and see them as an essential part of their lives, children will remain welcome 'obstacles' in competition for jobs and a tempting reason to avoid the rat race.[31]

Gender equality is clearly and rightly endorsed in the impersonal, public domain, yet the interaction between the realm of employment and the home is not simple. The desires and dynamics of the 'society of two' are a separate world. This world is not built upon impersonal bureaucratic structures, but upon ' . . . judgements intrinsic to the household economy as a social space that is organized and sustained through reciprocity and gift-exchange.'[32] Equality in this sphere requires an elaborate set of discernments in which personality

differences and divergences in ability are important, nego-
tiation and cooperation ongoing. In this 'society of two',
reciprocity and long-term equilibrium is much more
important than strict, literal or limited notions of equality.
Yet the achievement of balance and reciprocity rooted in trust,
commitment and ongoing negotiation, so central to the fragile
existence of the couple, is constantly threatened by corrosive
external pressure, for example, that placed upon one partner
to relocate in order to maintain the progress of their career.

The tensions inherent in the picture of modern loving
painted by Beck and Beck-Gernsheim play out with particular
poignancy when it comes to children. In an economic
environment increasingly geared to dual career families, and
in a culture with diminished familial and communitarian ties
it is abundantly clear that children impoverish their parents.
Yet, of course, love of a child represents, even more than
conjugal love, the hope of being natural and authentic, of
leading a meaningful existence. In fact, it is difficult to match
the psychological utility that children bring: 'Having a child,
looking after it and providing for it can give life new meaning
and significance, can in fact become the very core of one's
private existence.'[33] This is especially the case in a world
in which relationships between couples are fragile. Unlike
partners, children cannot easily escape their parents and in
contemporary society the relationship between the gener-
ations seems to be less commonly driven by the needs of the
child for love and nurture, and more by the needs of the parent
for a substitute love object: 'The child becomes the final
alternative to loneliness, a bastion against the vanishing
chances of being loving and being loved.'[34]

Couple love as religion

In the light of the decline in influence of institutional forms of religion, and the stress upon the conjugal unit as *the* place where the individual 'finds' and fulfils herself or himself, Beck and Beck-Gernsheim have suggested that our faith in love as expressed in the man–woman relationship could perhaps be seen as a vehicle for religious experience, as a 'latter-day religion'. In a social world structured by the market, which places little value on traditional authority, the idea that the man–woman relationship might become the place where transcendence is experienced and meaning sought is quite plausible. The couple then becomes an alternative place of utopian yearnings where we experience 'communism without capitalism'[35] and to which we turn wearied by our cynical and disillusioned world to be re-enchanted. This suggestion, startling at first, should not perhaps surprise us, for as we noted in Chapter 2, there is a long and complex historical interaction between conjugal love and Christian faith beginning with the Old Testament marriage metaphor for the relationship between Yahweh and his people. One small but telling footnote to this complex history is that the industry in romantic fiction that is Mills and Boon has its direct historical origin with evangelical literature.[36] Furthermore, there are resonances in the world of contemporary religion. Martyn Percy in his analysis of the ecstatic worship characteristic of the Toronto Blessing and the vineyard churches makes a strong case for regarding such worship as 'sublimated eroticism'.[37]

Furthermore, the idea that love is akin to worship also has a robust sociological pedigree, rooted in the recognition by the influential French sociologist, Emile Durkheim (1858–1917), that there is a sacred dimension to human solidarity found in all face-to-face communities including the 'society of two'. Here, he argued, elements of ritual, moral obligation, self-sacrifice and self-transcendence could be found. In such a view the sacred is inherent in the genuinely erotic: sexual desire draws the individual through the process of 'falling in love' into a merging, into the 'society of two', rendering to erotic love an inherently transformative and ritual character which naturally generates through emotional bonding a personal and social bond, a 'conjugal' structure.[38] This reality can be seen clearly echoed in the way in which the idea of worship (the ascription of worth) almost always reserved for God, is used within the BCP marriage service, by the groom who promises: 'With my body I thee worship.'

More soberly, for the sociologist Randall Collins this understanding of the couple as implicated in each other helps to explain the darker side to relationships.[39] For, he argues, it is because sexual relationships like marriage are experienced as ritually constituted moral bonds that an intensity of violence, jealousy and hatred can be generated when one party feels that they have been betrayed. More rational parties to a 'pure relationship' would simply cut their losses and walk away, preparing themselves to move on to the next life-enhancing project.

No safe harbours

In this chapter we have considered two rival attempts to make sense of the revolution in the man–woman relationship that has unfolded over the last forty years. The more radical of these, that of Anthony Giddens, presents what is primarily a political account in which greater democracy is brought to our personal lives, especially for women. In this view, romantic love and the institution of marriage are cultural products tied to inequality between the sexes – their demise is to be embraced. Such a portrayal, which envisages a sharp break with the past, seems consistent with the statistical data on trends in marriage, divorce and cohabitation that demonstrate dramatic change over the period. Even the vocabulary associated with marriage has a decidedly 'old-fashioned' feel about it: 'husband' and 'wife' and more particularly their precursors 'bachelor' and 'spinster' are labels which immediately conjure the gender expectations and roles of yesteryear. By contrast, the idea of the 'pure relationship' with its emphasis on individual autonomy and the maintenance of difference within a couple has a contemporary ring of prudence about it: it feels more 'realistic'. Such a relationship is perhaps especially attractive to those who perceive marriage to be an instrument of the State or indeed as inherently patriarchal, an institution in which women receive a 'raw deal', be it an unfair share of the domestic and child-care duties, less good health or the possibility of domestic violence or *de facto* rape. Furthermore, no one is forced into or trapped by such a pure relationship that can be dissolved without many of the costs – social, legal and (if Giddens is to be believed) emotional – entailed in the formal dissolution that is divorce. In short, then, the 'pure' relationship allows couples to be who they are without the historical or legal baggage that the 'institution' of marriage brings in its wake to a couple's relationship.

Whilst the idea of the 'pure relationship' casts a searing beam across the landscape of intimacy and does indeed highlight real tendencies in how many men and women approach sexual relationships, as a purely descriptive account it does not do real justice to the continuities that exist in our social world.

For the great majority of young people today, cohabitation is perceived as part of a greater horizon of aspiration. The fact that living together blurs the previous clear-cut distinctions between 'going steady', engagement and the early years of marriage does not make what lies at the heart of marriage – a lifelong sexually exclusive union – redundant. Nearly three-quarters of men and women under 35 who are childless and cohabiting anticipate getting married at some point, and one third of these have active plans to do so.[40] Despite the undoubted flight from the traditional, only 9 per cent of couples agree with the statement that 'there is no point getting married – it's only a piece of paper' whereas 59 per cent agree with the statement that 'even though it might not work out for some people, marriage is still the best kind of relationship.'[41] Thus whilst clearly evolving in character then, the ideal of marriage remains immensely important, despite significant changes in the ideas and practices concerned with its initiation. The persistence of this ideal runs counter to the model of personhood which lies at the centre of Giddens' analysis. I have suggested that this is in fact an economic model, that the partners to the 'pure relationship' are primarily consumers rather than citizens. The difficulty with this is that people entering relationships are happily more interested in consummation than consumption.

By contrast, for Beck and Beck-Gernsheim the expansion of economic rationality at the expense of traditional modes of thinking and acting is a hostile invasion that threatens the man–woman relationship. For them, far from love being reduced to a 'mask' or illusion, there is a powerful cultural desire to make of love a religion, to see in the other a 'soul mate' and in the couple a 'beloved community': a harbour safe from the relentless storms of everyday modern life and its pressures. Unfortunately, as they so clearly describe, that harbour is positioned in a very vulnerable location barely protected from the destructive forces of wave and wind. Furthermore it is not easily reached and, once found, the temptation to leave for a safer berth is great. Beck and Beck-Gernsheim therefore highlight the paradox of modern loving – the combination of fantasies about the possibilities of intimacy and the immense fragility for the man–woman relationship in a chaotic and risky social world. Yet their view of the couple as joined by a ritually constituted moral bond where the one belongs to the other by virtue of erotic embodiment has a clear sacramental resonance with the central Christian concept of the 'one flesh'.

The 'piece of paper', as the institution of marriage is so often reductively described and derided, does still retain real social and psychological weight within our world. Yet the Christian idea of marriage is under real threat, not from the practice of cohabitation, which as a transitional stage could be incorporated into a modified understanding of how contemporary marriage might legitimately be formed, but from a combination of two forces: an ethic of soulless despair which reduces sexuality to the purely hedonistic and denounces mutuality and commitment in the name of individual autonomy, and from the unrealistic expectations placed upon the couple relationship by the atrophying of other social bonds in our chaotic and fluid world. The challenge to the Church is whether it can craft a response to a rapidly changing consumerist culture; a response that supports and equips men and women for the task that the journey of marriage in our modern world requires.

CHAPTER SIX

Come live with me and be my love

This has been a book about marriage and at the heart of the marriage relationship lies an invitation to 'come and be my love', to love and be loved: an invitation that issues from desire, rendering the speaker vulnerable and affirming the beloved. As such it is rooted and participates in the nature of love which is God. Such an invitation is not issued lightly, indeed few of us make a more serious request to embrace otherness, with all the unknowable consequences for our own development as persons, in the course of our lives. It is, then, an invitation that the Church should engage with thoroughly if it wishes to assist people in making marriage a project for life rather than colluding with a contemporary secular individualism which trashes the hopes and dreams for successful unions 'betwixt a man and a woman' by confining them to a series of ever-changing life-projects.

Yet the poetic line, 'Come live with me and be my love', is one that is fraught with ambiguity. Originally the opening invitation of a piece of courtly pastoralism by Marlowe, 'The Passionate Shepherd to his Love', which circulated widely in polite circles of the seventeenth century, it generated, at least three prominent 'answers'.[1] Of these, the one I wish to evoke is that of John Donne's satirical response, 'The Baite', which drags the fantasy of courtly love through a literalisation of the metaphor that love with its 'silver hook' is a snare, to the riverbank itself and the reality of fishing – involving as it does the cold, the uncomfortable and the act of killing for consumption. The idyll of pastoral love, Donne suggests, can only exist as part of the games courtiers play; the actual experience of everyday marriage is much more grounded. Likewise, contemporary accounts and aspirations for the couple relationship, like that advocated by Anthony Giddens, which suggest that its essential nature is as a free association, devoid of the institutional aspects attendant upon a sustained emotional bond, have to be unmasked for what they so often are: convenient, egotistical and utilitarian.

The Church has a crucial role in assisting couples to acknowledge and ground their loving in a commitment that goes beyond a contract between two individuals,[2] in a way that speaks of the transcendent dimension of the human pair-bond, and which also provides a framework for everyday living. This is a massive task in our society, in which, despite the historically high rates of marital and relationship break-down, aspiration for a lifelong harmonious and intimate union have not been abandoned. Rather, there has been an increased idealisation of the couple. Such highly valued relationships have then to be constructed 'against the odds' in a chaotic social world devoid of secure traditions, where great emphasis and value is also placed upon individual fulfilment.

This challenge is usually addressed by the Church through the pastoral 'hook' that the marriage service provides, and the ritual itself can communicate such messages with a high degree of effectiveness. However, this engagement on the part of the Church does require people to get married, and to do so in a church building. Until comparatively recently the majority of marriages in Britain were initiated in a religious ceremony. Indeed a decade ago in 1991, 51 per cent of people marrying for the first time did so within a religious context; by the year 2000 that figure had fallen significantly, to 36 per cent.[3] Whilst such decline is part of a long-standing trend, its acceleration is no doubt due to the 1994 Marriage Act which allowed civil weddings to be conducted at approved venues, usually somewhat more attractive venues than the average registry office.[4]

The world of weddings is a market, and an increasingly deregulated one; if the Church of England wishes to retain influence within it, it needs to take a hard look at its structures and the associated restrictions. Getting married is, among other things, an act of celebration, and many couples, hesitant but initially desirous of a Christian ceremony, find the Church's bureaucracy and rules inaccessible and off-putting. The Church then needs to act boldly and swiftly in this highly fluid and rapidly changing situation to fight for its 'market share' against the commercial forces that would seek to turn every celebration of marriage into a themed, and expensive, extravaganza. Reform of the rules governing marriage within the Anglican parochial system are important but, as I have suggested in this essay, the Church also needs to conduct a major rethink in its approach to cohabitation.

Let me briefly suggest three ways in which the Church might seek to do this:

1. Abandon an undiscriminating opposition to premarital sex.
2. Acknowledge a role for cohabitation as part of the process of becoming married.
3. Broaden the Church's engagement from the wedding to the marriage.

1. Abandon an undiscriminating opposition to premarital sex

The Church now accepts, promotes and, broadly speaking, shares with the surrounding culture an understanding of sexuality which derives its meaning primarily from the context of interpersonal love rather than from its potential link to procreation. Perhaps inevitably, a society with such an understanding of sexuality is much less likely to be prescriptive about its boundaries than if sex were linked directly to the possibility of new human life. In this latter scenario, the dominant one throughout history, there is, of course, a strong rationale for sexual intercourse being restricted to a permanent relationship between a man and a woman, as sexual partners are equally parents in the making. That is simply not the case today.

As it stands, the Church insists that sex before marriage, by which it means (if pushed to define it) penetrative sex, is wrong. Indeed the timbre of Church pronouncements in recent years has, in this regard, been defensive and cautious, seeking to address the nation with authoritative, firm and traditional teaching aimed at upholding the 'sanctity of marriage'. This tendency is exemplified by the House of Bishops' recent teaching document *Marriage*, in which it states that that 'sexual intercourse, as an expression of faithful intimacy, properly belongs with marriage *exclusively*.'[5] The difficulty is, of course, that the Church has failed in the contemporary context to articulate a clear rationale for this opposition to intimate sexual expression outside marriage. It simply doesn't make sense to most people when the average age at marriage is about 30 and highly effective contraception is readily available. Such a failure also reflects, I would suggest, at least in part, a lack of conviction from within the Christian community itself. Conservative movements like the prominent US 'True Love Waits' campaign have not been seriously advocated nor do they even find a resonance in mainstream Anglican Church life. In light of this, the approach taken in *Marriage* is not without its dangers. For as David Pailin has pointed out:

... the Achilles' heel of attempts to impose views based on cultural and institutional inheritance is the brute stubbornness of what is experienced. Reality is not what we decide that it is; in the end illusions and delusions are exposed for what they are'.[6]

The bishops' teaching document, whilst it might reassure an older generation of churchgoers, fails in this regard to address its main constituency, for it seeks to answer questions that only the most conservative and sectarian within the Church are posing. It is seen, then, as largely irrelevant to many who might otherwise seek its guidance, and the Church's continued emphasis on the undesirability of sexual intercourse before marriage is merely perceived as part of a broader institutional fixation upon sexuality. Worse still, by continuing to promote as an ideal a stance which few can seriously justify, and to which less than 1 per cent of those getting married actively adheres, the Church implicitly brackets together sexual activity that takes place within a *de facto* marital relationship and the wildest excesses of promiscuity. Sexuality is a powerful drive, which is why every human society seeks to control and channel this instinct. Yet in the late twentieth century as a result of contraceptive innovation and family planning, there has been an increased utilisation of sexual experience for purely hedonistic or even commercial ends, which should be a matter of some considerable concern to Christians. In this context, Church leaders need to adopt a more discriminating approach to sexuality. The emphasis on sexual chastity, which places all the moral significance upon an act – the initiation of sexual practice, and has, for example, little or no interest in the character of marital sexuality[7] – should give way as the touchstone of Christian sexual ethics to a conception of sexual integrity, where the emphasis is more firmly person-centred and contextual. Thus, the Christian community needs to find ways of affirming and celebrating the genuinely erotic. So that what an earlier Anglican report described as the 'polyphony of love' which 'finds expression in the lovers' bodily union,'[8] that is a more holistic person-centred account of sexuality, can be seen for what it is: a more attractive and persuasive understanding of sexuality than the instrumental and reductive ones that circulate so widely. Such a holistic vision for sexuality would affirm sexual expression where it was linked to emotional intimacy and genuine commitment.

Indeed, it could be argued that the Christian community should be enormously happy if the only category of sexual activity that occurred outside of marriage was genuinely pre-marital, that is between people who subsequently got married. If the Church wishes to retain or, indeed re-establish, influence with many of its more peripheral members it might admit as much. Indeed, it might even go further and regard sexual expression between a couple in an exclusive relationship, which possessed depth and quality and was open to the possibility of marriage at some point in the future, as acceptable. For whilst it continues with an undiscriminating approach to sexuality against the backdrop of a complete collapse in the plausibility of religiously based prohibitions on premarital sexual expression[9] within Western society, it undermines its authority when its chooses to speak out against premature or promiscuous, casual or coercive uses of sexuality.

2. Acknowledge a role for cohabitation as part of the process of becoming married

Cohabitation of the young is now an integral part of the courtship process; it is not a passing phenomenon and some recently ordained clergy may not have had the experience of preparing a couple for marriage who are not already living together. Cohabitation blurs the previously clear distinction between courtship and marriage and is seen by some to provide many of the benefits of marriage without its perceived risks. That perception is, of course, misleading for it is rooted in the misapprehension that not to make a commitment is not to take a risk. Yet imagining the future is one of the defining human characteristics and for men and women in long-term relationships truly to flourish requires an explicit commitment to the long term. Lack of such commitment breeds a nagging insecurity that ultimately undermines the relationship. For most people in our culture, that explicit commitment is most clearly expressed through 'getting married'.

Yet, as we have noted, today love between a man and a woman is conducted in a chaotic climate, in a culture marked by a 'push-pull' attitude to marriage. For widespread cohabitation and high levels of divorce coexist with a strong affirmation of the ideal of marriage, expressed in the highly negative response people give to the question 'Is marriage an outdated institution?' This tension reflects the great aspirations that today's men and women have of their relationships, and especially of the emotional quality of their personal life. Such an emphasis is to be welcomed, celebrated and affirmed. Yet marriage is for the everyday: it is concerned with the art of the possible. Whilst the bishops' document *Marriage* refers to people being misled by 'fantasies about sex', concern could equally be expressed about the fantastic expectations associated with emotional intimacy. Just as Thomas More's political *Utopia* is literally a 'no-place', so too is the state of the 'perfect marriage'. The quest to find the perfect soul mate is a doomed and destructive one.

In the light of the widespread and accurate apprehension that modern marriage is 'not easy' and the high levels of divorce which support this, young people have good reason to be hesitant about making the commitment to marriage. In choosing to live together in the first instance, however, the

[handwritten margin note: WHAT ABOUT THE BIBLE'S ATTITUDE TO MARRIAGE — THERE IS LITTLE TO COMMENT IT]

[120]

expectation and hope of many, not always articulated, is that this provisional commitment will deepen into something more permanent. The rapid spread and the relatively quick acceptance of 'living together' in the 1980s and 1990s does not, I believe, signal an abandonment of the ideal of Christian marriage, but an evolution in how it is initiated. In the light of the diversity of Christian marriage practices in the past, the Church might exercise caution in continuing to wed itself to a relatively recent understanding of marriage, which places undue emphasis on its legal and bureaucratic dimensions. If the Church's business is to facilitate and encourage people to flourish and grow in love, not least in conjugal love, then it needs to craft a positive, creative and generous response to cohabitation.

A starting point for such engagement would be a recognition that despite the pejorative language often employed (like 'shacking up', 'living in sin'), deciding to live with someone, especially if it entails a mortgage, is a serious step. If entering an intimate relationship is like learning to swim, then marrying directly is jumping in the deep end of a swimming pool, and cohabitation is the more gradual approach from the shallow end. This latter approach involves feeling what the experience might be like, with one's feet firmly planted upon the ground and edging slowly out. However, there comes a point when the bottom of the pool begins to slope away and a decision has to be made: commitment is required. Many contemporary relationships have this dynamic: a prudent but cautious movement towards a permanent commitment. Cohabitation, then, is a question which seeks and desires an affirmative response, but allows for the possibility of walking away. Such walking away, however, is not in psychological or emotional terms a casual act – the limbs move heavily, as it were, through the water. If the Church recognised cohabitation as an integral and legitimate part of the journey from courtship to marriage, it would then have the opportunity to promote a sense of direction within relationships and could encourage couples to think seriously about their future together, prompting a deeper commitment. The alternative is that it continues to 'opt out' of a sphere of potential influence, thereby increasing the possibility of people drifting from one relationship to another. Rather than shouting from the edge of the pool then, like some authoritarian parent, advocating a 'deep end' theology of marriage, the Christian community could be 'up to its neck' sharing the genuine difficulties men and women face today and grounding the Church more securely in the everyday domestic world.

3. Broaden the focus from the wedding to the marriage

Churches need then to explore ways of engaging with the journey into the absolute commitment that the marriage vows entail through a deeper appreciation of its experiential contours. The parallels with the Christian spiritual journey, including its institutional aspects (e.g. baptism, confirmation), are straightforward, extensive and a considerably under-used resource. If a period of living together before legal marriage came to be seen as a natural part of the process of becoming married, the marriage service itself could be more consciously re-conceived to meet this reality, becoming an act of celebration and confirmation, rather than of registration and initiation. But pastoral connection with couples should not be signed off with the handing over of the marriage certificate. For the couple, relationship is a fundamental dimension of everyday life, the primary place where the transcendent is encountered through the love of another; where the formation of moral character occurs; and where far-reaching decisions relating to the conception, nurture and socialisation of children and the nature and rationale of employment, voluntary or paid, are made and reflected upon. This is the arena in which couples struggle to determine what equality in a relationship might mean; work out how to achieve a balance between the conflicting demands of being a parent, a partner and a person; discern how to navigate the transitions of life or the characteristic stages of marriage; and face the challenge of maintaining intimacy over decades of living together. The Church then needs to grasp a vocation for the articulation and advocacy of a marital spirituality which encounters the 'brute stubbornness' of married life and seeks to help men and women and children flourish within it.

NOTES

Chapter 1. **Facing the challenge**

1. The headline was in response to two publications: Gary Jenkins, *Cohabitation: A Biblical Perspective*, Grove Ethical Studies no 84 (Bramcote: Grove Books Ltd, 1992) and Duncan J. Dormor, *The Relationship Revolution: Cohabitation, Marriage and Divorce in Contemporary Europe* (London: One plus One, 1992).

2. Board for Social Responsibility, *Something to Celebrate: Valuing Families in Church and Society* (London: Church House Publishing, 1999), p. 118.

3. The report from the Board for Social Responsibility was undeservedly savaged by Michael Banner in an article in the *Church Times*, 'Nothing to Declare', *Church Times* 16 June 1995, for lack of theological rigour. In the sense that some theologians can, Banner 'shouts': 'The voice that has been lost is the voice of a Church which sees the world in the light of what it knows to be the decisive Word of God, Jesus Christ. The voice it speaks with is inevitably the one that already sounds most loudly in our culture: the voice of Western, bourgeois liberalism.' Archbishop George Carey also voiced his criticism in General Synod decrying the report for a lack of advocacy for the 'biblical ideal'. Whilst such criticisms are not entirely unjustified, the tenor of the response provides a clear example of the Church's inclination to retreat from the world and engage in 'fiddling around in "Bible land" as the world burns.' (Terrence W. Tilley, 'Incommensurablity, Intratextuality, and Fideism', *Modern Theology* 5:2: 87–111, 1989) p. 95.

4. House of Bishops, *Marriage: a teaching document from the House of Bishops of the Church of England* (London: Church House Publishing, 1999).

5. Ibid. p. 8, my emphasis.

6. Ibid. p. 11.

7. By 'cohabitation' I refer to: a man and a woman living together

[124]

within a sexual union without that union having been formalised in either a civil or religious ceremony. I will not consider the vexed question of same-sex relationships within this book, though I do believe that the approach taken here to sexual ethics is consistent with a view that sees gay marriage as a natural and reasonable extension of the Christian tradition. See: Gareth Moore, *A Question of Truth: Christianity and Homosexuality* (London: Continuum, 2003); Eugene Rogers Jr., *Sexuality and the Christian Body* (Oxford: Blackwell, 1999); and, Jeffery John *Permanent, Faithful, Stable* (London: DLT, 2000).

8. By the Lutheran sociologist, Peter Berger. See: Berger, *The Heretical Imperative: Contemporary Possibilities of Religious Affirmation* (London: Collins, 1980) p. 13.

9. Anthony E. Harvey, *Promise of Pretence: A Christian's Guide to Sexual Morals* (London: SCM, 1994); Kenneth W. Stevenson, *To Join Together: The Rite of Marriage Studies in the Reformed Rites of the Catholic Church* (New York: Pueblo Publishing, 1992); Adrian Thatcher, *Living Together and Christian Ethics* (Cambridge: Cambridge University Press, 2002) and Jack Dominian, 'Marriage under threat' pp. 444–449 in Charles E. Curran and Richard McCormick (eds), *Readings in Moral Theology 8: Dialogue about Catholic Sexual Teaching* (New York: Mahwah, 1993).

10. 'At the risk of unconstructive carping, one must ask whether, if "the betrothal solution" were taken up as positive church policy and provided with forms of service of its own, it might prove to be one more hurdle people would have to be persuaded to jump, since by definition they are not yet willing to make a formal commitment?' Helen Oppenheimer, review of *Living Together and Christian Ethics* (Thatcher) in *Theology* CV No 827, 396.

11. John Gillis, *For Better, For Worse: British Marriages, 1600 to the Present* (Oxford: Oxford University Press, 1980).

12. Jack Dominian, *Passionate and Compassionate Love: A Vision for Christian Marriage* (London: DLT, 1991) p. 173.

13. E.g. John Haskey, 'Pre-marital cohabitation and the probability of subsequent divorce: analyses using new data from the General Household Survey', *Population Trends* 68, (London: The Stationery Office, 1992), 10–19.

14. John Haskey, 'Cohabitational and marital histories of adults in Great Britain', *Population Trends*, 96, (London: The Stationery Office, 1999), 13–24.

15. A recent survey of young people found that a mere 4 per cent agreed with the statement: 'Marriage is old fashioned and no longer

relevant' and 89 per cent stated that they would like to get married in the future. See: The Opinion Research Business, *Young People's Lives in Britain Today*, (London: The Opinion Research Business, 2000).

Chapter 2. Not in the passion of lust

1. Though this is less frequently the case when love between men or between women is under consideration. In such cases churches often adopt a much more reductive approach in which sexual desire is about selfish pleasure rather than mutual giving in love. See, for example, Gareth Moore, *A Question of Truth: Christianity and Homosexuality* (London: Continuum, 2003), especially Chapter 2.
2. *Book of Common Prayer* (1549, 1552, 1662).
3. This sentiment has a venerable history reaching back through Aquinas and Jerome to its origins in the second-century Pythagorean philosopher, Sextus. For comment on John Paul II's remark on October 8 see Peter Nichols, *The Pope's Divisions: the Roman Catholic Church Today* (London: Faber and Faber, 1981).
4. Stoicism was one of the most popular philosophical systems of the Roman and Hellenistic period. Founded in the third century by the Greek philosopher Zeno it continued into the third century AD. Prominent Stoic philosophers of the early Christian period included Seneca and Marcus Aurelius. The Stoics believed that the universe was underpinned and guided by *logos*, a reason, which might be understood as Nature, God, fate or providence. The Stoics argued that individuals should act according to this *logos* adopting a disposition of passionlessness and not, for example, regretting unavoidable pain or suffering.
5. 'A powerful "fantasy of the loss of vital spirit" lay at the root of many late classical attitudes to the male body. It is one of the many notions that gave male continence a firm foothold in the folk wisdom of the world in which Christian celibacy would soon be preached.' Peter Brown, *The Body and Society: Men, Women, and Sexual Renunciation in Early Christianity* (New York: Columbia University Press, 1988), p. 19.
6. See Peter Brown in Paul Veyne (ed), *A History of Private Life I: From Pagan Rome to Byzantium* (Harvard University Press: London, 1987).
7. From the discourse *On Sex*. The teachings and discourses of Musonius Rufus were reported by a wide range of his contemporaries, most prominently, an unidentified writer called Lucius.
8. Roman understanding of the social consequences that flowed from sexual actions can be clearly seen in the Augustus legislation *Lex*

Julia de adulteriis (18 BC). Here a distinction is drawn between adultery, extra-marital sexual relations with or by a married woman, and illicit sexual relations *(stuprum)* which might include sexual relations with an unmarried virgin, widow or boy of respectable status. Both offences were punishable by the law, with adultery considered the greater offence. Sexual relations with slaves, prostitutes or others below the threshold of respectability were not covered by any legislation. Despite strong opposition to the double standard between the sexes in theological teaching and ethical exhortation, the legal definition of adultery, as extramarital relations with or by a respectable married woman, did not change under the Christian emperors of the late classical period.

9. Brown, 1987, p. 251.
10. In Book III.7.57 of the *Stromata* (Miscellanies), Clement writes: 'The human ideal of continence, I mean that which is set forth by Greek philosophers, teaches that one should fight desire and not be subservient to it so as to bring it to practical effect. But our ideal is not to experience desire at all. Our aim is not that while a man feels desire he should get the better of it, but that he should be continent even respecting desire itself. This chastity cannot be attained in any other way except by God's grace.' (Roberts-Donaldson English Translation).

    See *http://www.earlychristianwritings.com/clement.html* for further information.
11. Sadly we only know Julian's views through extensive quotation in his opponents' writings.
12. *Contra Julianum* III, xiv, 28 quoted in Brown, 1988, p. 391.
13. Quoted in Eric J. Carlson, *Marriage and the English Reformation* (Oxford: Blackwell, 1994), p. 56.
14. Carlson, 1994, p. 76.
15. See Diarmaid MacCulloch, *Thomas Cranmer* (London: Yale University Press, 1996), pp. 421–2.
16. Jeremy Taylor, *Holy Living* (1650), quoted in *Love's Redeeming Work: the Anglican Quest for Holiness* compiled by Geoffrey Rowell, Kenneth Stevenson and Rowan Williams (Oxford: Oxford University Press, 2001), p. 205.
17. See Derrick Sherwin Bailey, *The Mystery of Love and Marriage* (London: SCM, 1952) p. 65.
18. *Marriage and the Church's Task* (London: CIO Publishing, 1978), pp. 33–34.
19. Bailey, 1952, p. 44.
20. Blu Greenberg in Kieran Scott and Michael Warren (eds),

Perspectives on Marriage: A Reader second edition (Oxford: Oxford University Press, 2001), p. 426.

21. See, for example, Luke 20:34–36: 'And Jesus said to them, "The sons of this age marry and are given in marriage, but those who are accounted worthy to attain to that age and to the resurrection from the dead neither marry nor are given in marriage, for they cannot die anymore, because they are equal to angels and are sons of God, being sons of the resurrection." '

22. The Greek in question is: εχέτω, which is translated as 'have' is used throughout the septuagint (the Greek version of the Old Testament) to mean 'have sexually'. See Gordon D. Fee, *The First Epistle to the Corinthians* NICNT (Grand Rapids: Eerdmans, 1987), p. 278.

23. For example: 'When there is a genuine imbalance in how much sex you both need, it is necessary to compromise. One of the best ways to do this is to agree when you will make love – say, once a week. To make the agreement work, the one with the higher sex drive must undertake not to ask for sex at any other time. The one with the lower sex drive has to agree to participate fully and willingly on the agreed date. Both must concentrate on making the experience good for each other and themselves.' *The Relate Guide to Sex in Loving Relationships* (London: Vermilion, 1992), p. 152.

24. *Berakoth* ii. 5. See Greenberg, 2001, p. 429 for a fuller account.

25. See Fee, 1987, and C. K. Barrett, *A Commentary on the First Epistle of the Corinthians* (New York: HNTC, 1968).

26. Fee, 1987, p. 280.

27. Barrett, 1968, p. 155.

28. The name given to the related epistles of 1 and 2 Timothy, and Titus, regarded by the majority of contemporary scholars as post-Pauline, dating from c. AD 100.

29. Octavio Paz, *The Double Flame: Essays on Love and Eroticism* (London: Haverill, 1996), p. 64.

Chapter 3: Just like everyone else

1. Edward Schillebeeckx, *Marriage: Human Reality and Sacred Mystery* (London: Sheed and Ward, 1976), p. xxviii.

2. Lawrence Stone, *The Family, Sex and Marriage in England 1500–1800* (London: Penguin, 1979), p. 29.

3. From chapter 12 of Aristotle, *The Nichomachean Ethics*, trans. J. A. K. Thomson (London: Penguin, 1953), p. 251.

4. Ulpian, *Digesta Iustiniani 1.1.1.3*, ed. Theodore Mommsen (Berlin, 1870).

5. Miriam Peskowitz, 'Family/ies in Antiquity: Evidence from Tan-

naitic Literature and Roman Galilean Architecture' in Shaye Cohen (ed), *The Jewish Family in Antiquity*, Brown Judaic Studies 289, (Atlanta: Scholar's Press 1993), p. 10.

6. At first blush the evidence is not supportive: one major world faith – Islam permits men up to four wives; there are some examples of polyandry (a woman marrying more than one husband) several African tribes practise a gerontocracy which precludes younger men from marrying and leads to high levels of polygyny; and, even the hero-kings of the Old Testament, David and Solomon appear to have had all too numerous wives. More systematically, the most extensive survey conducted on a wide range of human societies and their marriage systems, that of Murdock's *Ethnographic Atlas* (Pittsburgh: University of Pittsburgh Press, 1967), which considered 862 cultural groups, classifies a mere 16 per cent of societies as exclusively monogamous with the rest permitting polygyny. This is however a rather superficial analysis, for although the vast majority of societies permit polygyny, only 5 to 10 per cent of men actually have several wives simultaneously. This is certainly Murdock's own conclusion: 'An impartial observer . . . would be compelled to characterise nearly every known human society as monogamous, despite the preference for and frequency of polygyny in the overwhelming majority' (pp. 27–28).

7. Penny Mansfield and Jean Collard, *The Beginning of the Rest of your Life?* (Basingstoke: Macmillan, 1988), p. 59.

8. Edward Shorter, *The Making of the Modern Family* (New York, 1975); Philippe Ariès, *Centuries of Childhood: A Social History of Family Life* (New York, 1979 [1962]); and Stone 1979, above.

9. Stone, 1979, p. 5.

10. Jack Goody, *The European Family: An Historico-Anthropological Essay* (Oxford: Blackwell Publishing, 2000), p. 4. Furthermore he continues: 'The care of children within a conjugal relationship which is defined by relatively exclusive sexual and marital rights is a quasi-universal.'

11. See Helen Oppenheimer, *Marriage* (London: Mowbray, 1990), p. 8ff.

12. Kenneth Stevenson, 'The Marriage Service' pp. 51–61 of Michael Perham (ed), *Liturgy 2000* (London: SPCK/Alcuin Club, 1991), p. 60.

13. Judith Evans Grubbs, ' "Pagan" and "Christian" Marriage: The State of the Question' *Journal of Early Christian Studies*, 2:3, 1994, 361–412 (p. 372).

14. Philip Reynolds, *Marriage in the Western Church: The Christianization of Marriage during the Patristic and Early Medieval Period* (Leiden: E. J. Brill, 1994), p. 333.

NOTES

15. Tal Ilan, 'Premarital Cohabitation in Ancient Judea: The Evidence of the Babatha Archive and the Mishnah (*Ketubbot 1.4*)' *Harvard Theological Review* 86:3, 1993, pp. 247–264.
16. For a clear contemporary account of the honour/shame complex see the ethnography of the Awlad 'Ali by Lila Abu-Lughod, *Veiled Sentiments: Honour and Poetry in a Bedouin Society* (Berkeley: University of California, 1986).
17. Reynolds, 1994, p. 35.
18. Ibid. p. 36.
19. Grubbs, 1994, p. 375.
20. Ignatius of Antioch, *Epistle to Polycarp 5:2*, trans. William R. Schoedel, *Ignatius of Antioch: A Commentary on the letters of Ignatius of Antioch* (Philadelphia: Fortress Press, 1985).
21. See Kenneth Stevenson, *Nuptial Blessing* (London: Alcuin Club/ SPCK, 1982).
22. Reynolds, 1994, p. 315.
23. Kenneth Stevenson, 'Van Gennep and Marriage – Strange Bedfellows: A Fresh Look at the Rites of Marriage', pp. 110–133 in Stevenson, *Wonderful and Sacred Mystery* (Washington: The Pastoral Press, 1992), p. 129.
24. See John Gillis, *For Better, For Worse: British Marriages, 1600 to the Present* (Oxford: Oxford University Press, 1980). Also, Stone states that before 1750, marriage could be entered by a 'bewildering variety of ways' (1979, p. 29).
25. Ibid. p. 47.
26. Ibid. pp. 179–180.
27. Horace Walpole, *Memoirs*, vol. 1, p. 340. Quoted in Stephen Parker *Informal Marriage, Cohabitation and the Law, 1760–1989* (Basingstoke: Macmillan, 1990).
28. See Gillis, 1980.
29. Including Patricia Morgan, *Marriage-Lite: The Rise of Cohabitation and its Consequences* (London: Institute for the Study of Civil Society, 2000) and Edward Pratt, *Living in Sin?* (Southsea: St Simon's Church, 1994).
30. HMSO, *Social Trends 31* (London: HMSO, 2001), p. 45.
31. David Ford and Dan Hardy, *Jubilate: Theology in Praise* (London: DLT, 1984), p. 144.
32. Kenneth Stevenson, 'The Marriage Service' in *Liturgy 2000*, ed. Michael Perham (London: SPCK, 1991), p. 59.
33. An important recent initiative has been the production of a detailed evaluation of current Church practice, published as *Church Support of Marriage and Adult Relationships in Southern England, 2003*,

produced by the Roehampton Social Research Unit, University of Surrey as a part of a joint venture between the Lord Chancellor's Department and Guildford Diocese.

34. House of Bishops, *Marriage: a teaching document from the House of Bishops of the Church of England* (London: Church House Publishing, 1999), p. 1.

Chapter 4: Ever since the Sixties

1. Augustine, *The Good of Marriage* V.5., David Hunter, (Trans) *Marriage in the Early Church* (Minneapolis :Fortress Press, 1992), p. 106.

2. Similar and simultaneous change has occurred across most of Europe. See Duncan Dormor, 'Marriage, and the Second Demographic Transition in Europe: A Review', in Adrian Thatcher (ed), *Celebrating Christian Marriage* (Edinburgh: T & T Clark, 2001).

3. Compiled from several issues of *Population Trends* (London: The Stationery Office).

4. See John Haskey, 'Divorce and Remarriage in England and Wales' *Population Trends* 95:18–22 (London: The Stationery Office, 1999).

5. See Francis Fukuyama, *The Great Disruption: Human Nature and the Reconstitution of Social Order* (New York: Free Press, 1999). Also: Duncan J. Dormor, *The Relationship Revolution: Cohabitation, Marriage and Divorce in Contemporary Europe* (London: One plus One, 1992).

6. Callum G. Brown, *The Death of Christian Britain* (London: Routledge, 2001), p. 1.

7. Brown, 2001, p. 2.

8. See Grace Davie, *Religion in Britain since 1945: Believing without Belonging* (Oxford: Blackwell, 1994).

9. Gillis, 1985, p. 289.

10. Brown, 2001, p. 8.

11. Lorna Sage, *Bad Blood* (London: Fourth Estate, 2001), pp. 175, 174.

12. Brown, 2001, p. 176.

13. *The Problem of Homosexuality* (London: CIO 1954); *Abortion : An Ethical Dilemma* (London: CIO 1965); and, *Putting Asunder: A Divorce Law for Contemporary Society* (London: SPCK, 1966).

14. Anthony Giddens, *Modernity and Self-Identity* (Cambridge: Polity Press, 1991), p. 82.

15. Gwynn Davis and Mervyn Murch, *Grounds for Divorce* (Basingstoke: Macmillan, 1988).

16. *Housekeeping Monthly,* 13 May 1951.

17. A. H. Halsey 'Further and Higher Education' pp. 221–253, in A. H.

Halsey with Josephine Webb (eds), *Twentieth-Century British Social Trends* (Basingstoke: Macmillan, 2000), pp. 231–232.

18. Halsey, 2000, pp. 291–292.

19. A repeated finding – see: Jacqueline Scott, Michael Braun and Duane Alwin, 'Partner, Parent and Worker: Family and Gender-Roles' in Roger Jowell, John Curtice, Alison Park, Lindsay Brook, Katarina Thomson and Caroline Bryson (eds), *British Social Attitudes: European Report* (Aldershot: Ashgate, 1998), pp. 19–37.

20. Kathleen Kiernan, 'The respective roles of men and women in Tomorrow''s Europe' paper given at the International Conference: *Human Resources in Europe at the dawn of the 21st century*, pp. 27–29, Luxembourg Government: Eurostat, 1991 (p 21).

21. Penny Mansfield, Fiona McAllister and Jean Collard, 'Equality: Implications for sexual intimacy in marriage.' *Sexual and Marital Therapy* 7.2, 1992, 213–220 (pp. 217, 219).

22. Fiona McAllister, Penny Mansfield and Duncan Dormor, 'Expectations and Experiences of Marriage Today' *Journal of Social Work Practice* 5:181–191, 1991, (p. 190).

23. See Geoffery Gorer, *Exploring English Character* (London: The Cresset Press, 1955); Stephen Harding, David Phillips and Michael Fogarty, *Contrasting Values in Western Europe* (Basingstoke: Macmillan, 1986); European Values Survey Group, *European Values Study*, Unpublished tabulated results (Gallup Poll Ltd).

24. John R. Gillis, *For Better, For Worse: British Marriages, 1600 to the Present* (Oxford: OUP, 1985), p. 318.

25. *Lambeth Conference 1930* (London: SPCK, 1930) Resolution 41, p. (1) 327.

26. *Lambeth Conference 1958* (London: SPCK, 1958) Resolution 115.

27. Peter Berger, *The Heretical Imperative: Contemporary Possibilities of Religious Affirmation* (London: Collins, 1980), p. 13.

28. Helen Oppenheimer, *Marriage* (London: Mowbray, 1990), p. 3.

29. Dirk J. van de Kaa 'Europe's Second Demographic Transition', *Population Bulletin* 42:1 (1987).

30. Henri Leridon, Yves Charbit, Philippe Collomb, Jean-Paul Sardon and Laurent Toulemon, *La Seconde Révolution Contraceptive*, Institut National d'Etudes Demographiques Travaux et Documents Cahiers No. 117 (Paris: Presses Universitaires de France, 1987).

31. Ansley Coale and Susan C. Watkins, *The Decline of Fertility in Europe* (Princeton: Princeton University Press, 1986), p. 435.

32. From the marriage service of the *Book of Common Prayer* (1662).

33. Kaye Wellings, Julia Field, Anne Johnson and Jane Wadsworth, *Sexual Behaviour in Britain*, (London: Penguin, 1994), p. 48.

34. Compared with two in three brides marrying in the late 1950s. See: Karen Dunnell, *Family Formation 1976* (London: HMSO, 1979).

35. This figure relates to the proportion of women who married in 1996. See John Haskey 'Cohabitation in Great Britain: past, present and future trends – and attitudes' *Population Trends* 103 (London: The Stationery Office, 2001), pp. 4–25.

36. See Chris Shaw and John Haskey, 'New estimates and projections of the population cohabiting in England and Wales' *Population Trends* 95 (London: The Stationery Office, 1999), pp. 7–17.

37. Dirk J.van de Kaa, 'Options and Sequences: Europe's Demographic Patterns', *Journal of the Australian Population Association*, 14:1 (1997), 1–29 (p. 3).

38. John Haskey, 'Pre-marital cohabitation and the probability of subsequent divorce: analyses using new data from the General Household Survey' *Population Trends* 68 (London: The Stationery Office, 1992), pp. 10–19 and John Haskey, 'Cohabitational and marital histories of adults in Great Britain', *Population Trends* 96 (London: The Stationery Office, 1999), pp. 13–24.

39. Anne Barlow, Simon Duncan, Grace James and Alison Park, 'Just a piece of paper? Marriage and cohabitation', in Alison Park, John Curtice, Katerina Thomson, Lindsey Jarvis and Catherine Bromley (eds), *British Social Attitudes: The 18th Report* (London: Sage, 2001), p. 38.

40. ' . . . evidence from both attitudes and behaviour suggests that pre-marital cohabitation has become a distinct stage – perhaps becoming the modern equivalent of the courtship period or of 'going steady' Haskey, 2001, p. 11.

41. 'wanting to have/was having/had just had children' was the second most common reason given by couples, in 1994/1995, in explanation of their decision to marry after a period of cohabitation. Haskey, 1999.

42. For the maintenance of a stable population a birth rate (technically a TPFR – Time Period Fertility Rate) of 2.1 children per woman is required. Europe's equivalent rate is *circa* 1.5, that of Italy *circa* 1.2.

43. There is an extensive literature on this subject. For reviews see Jay Belsky, 'Children and Marriage', in Robin Fincham (ed), *The Psychology of Marriage* (New York: Guilford, 1990) and Matthew Sanders, Jan M. Nicholson and Frank J. Floyd, 'Couples' relationships and Children' in Kim Halford and Howard Markham (eds), *Clinical Handbook of Marriage and Couple Interventions* (Chichester: Wiley, 1997).

44. Ministerial Group on the Family, *Supporting Families: A Consultation Document* (London: HMSO, 1998).
45. That is, a couple who marry directly are as likely to get divorced as a couple who have cohabited beforehand. See Haskey, 1999, and Kathleen Kiernan 'Cohabitation in Western Europe' *Population Trends* 96 (London: The Stationery Office, 1999), pp. 13–24.
46. John Ermisch and Marco Francesconi, 'Marriage and Cohabitation', in R. Berthoud and J. Gershuny (eds), *Seven Years in the lives of British families* (Abingdon: Polity Press, 2000).
47. Patricia Morgan, *Marriage-Lite: The Rise of Cohabitation and Its Consequences* (London: Civitas: Institute for the Study of Civil Society, 2000).
48. For further discussion of the non/pre-nuptial distinction, see Adrian Thatcher, *Living Together and Christian Ethics* (Cambridge: Cambridge University Press, 2002).
49. Barbara Thornes and Jean Collard, *Who Divorces?* (London: Routledge and Kegan Paul, 1979).
50. Jessie Bernard, *The Future of Marriage* (New York: Bantam Books, 1972), pp. 87–88.
51. Zygmunt Bauman, *Liquid Love* (Cambridge: Polity, 2003), viii.

Chapter 5: Love in a chaotic climate
1. Anthony Giddens, *The Transformation of Intimacy: Sexuality, Love and Eroticism in Modern Societies* (Cambridge: Polity Press, 1992).
2. Ibid. p. 58.
3. Ibid. p. 63.
4. Ibid. p. 61.
5. Ibid. p. 182.
6. Ibid. p. 43.
7. Ibid. p. 147.
8. Ibid. p. 182.
9. Ibid. p. 189.
10. Jeffrey Weeks, 'The Sexual Citizen' in M. Featherstone (ed.), *Love and Eroticism* (London: Sage, 1999).
11. Ibid. p. 43.
12. Giddens, 1992, p. 156.
13. Philip Mellor and Chris Shilling, 'Confluent Love and the Cult of the Dyad: The Pre-contractual Foundations of Contractarian Sexual Relationships', in Jon Davies and Gerard Loughlin (eds), *Sex these Days: Essays on Theology, Sexuality and Society* (Sheffield: Sheffield Academic Press, 1997), p. 51.
14. Bernadette Bawin-Legros and Anne Gauthier, 'Regulation of

Intimacy and Love Semantics in Couples Living Apart Together', *International Review of Sociology* 11:1:39–46 (2001).

15. Baumann, 2003, p. 15–16.
16. *Marriage and the Church's Task* (London: CIO Publishing, 1978), pp. 33–34.
17. Oppenheimer, 1990, p. 32.
18. See Anna Moore, 'A Woman's Touch', *Observer Magazine*, 20/07/03.
19. Giddens, 1992, p. 62.
20. Volkmar Sigusch, 'The nonsexual revolution', *Archives of Sexual Behaviour*, 4:332–359 (1989) quoted in Baumann, 2003, p. 39.
21. Michel Houellebecq, *Atomised*, trans. Frank Wynne, (London: Vintage, 1999/2000), p. 168.
22. Mellor and Shilling, 1987, pp. 57–58.
23. See the website of the inventors of 'The Rules', Ellen Fein and Sherrie Schneider: http://www.therulesbook.com/index.html
24. John R. Gillis, *A World of Their own Making* (Harvard: Harvard University Press, 1996), p. 151.
25. Ulrich Beck and Elizabeth Beck-Gernsheim, *The Normal Chaos of Love* (Cambridge: Polity Press, 1995), p. 24.
26. Elizabeth Beck-Gernsheim, *Reinventing the Family* (Cambridge: Polity Press, 2002), p. 40.
27. Ibid. p. 41.
28. Beck and Beck-Gernsheim, 1995, p. 24.
29. Ibid. pp. 175–176.
30. David Matzo McCarthy, *Sex and Love in the Home: A Theology of the Household* (London: SCM, 2001), p. 64.
31. Beck and Beck-Gernsheim, 1995, p. 32.
32. McCarthy, 2001, p. 187.
33. Beck and Beck-Gernsheim, 1995, p. 107.
34. Ibid. p. 37.
35. Ibid. p. 176.
36. See Brown, 2001, p. 82.
37. Martyn Percy, *Power and the Church: Ecclesiology in an Age of Transition* (London: Mowbray, 1998), chapter 8.
38. This is described by Shilling and Mellor (1997): 'In Durkheimian terms, sexual relationships can be viewed as a form of effervescent sociality because they manifest a stimulation of emotions and passions immanent within bodies yet transcendent of each individual involved, and because they give rise to ritual practices and moral obligations which help and define and consolidate a sense of solidarity between the sexual partners.' Pp. 53–54.
39. Randall Collins, *Sociological Insight: An Introduction to*

Non-Obvious Sociology, second edition (Oxford: Oxford University Press, 1992), Chapter 5; *Sociology of Marriage and the Family* (Chicago: Nelson Hall Publishers, 1988).

40. According to the *British Household Survey 1998*, 30 per cent of men and 25 per cent of women plan to marry and a further 46 per cent of men and 46 per cent of women will 'probably get married at some point'; Jill Matheson and Penny Babb (eds), *Social Trends* (London: HMSO, 2002), p 43.

41. Anne Barlow, Simon Duncan, Grace James and Alison Park, 'Just a piece of paper? Marriage and cohabitation', in Alison Park, John Curtice, Katerina Thomson, Lindsey Jarvis and Catherine Bromley (eds), *British Social Attitudes: The 18th Report* (London: Sage, 2001), p. 38.

Chapter 6: Come live with me and be my love

1. From Sir Walter Raleigh, John Donne and Cecil. D. Lewis.
2. The inclusion of a declaration by the community supporting the couple within the wedding service of *Common Worship* liturgy is to be welcomed in this regard.
3. Two-thirds of such are conducted within the Church of England.
4. John Haskey, 'Marriages in approved premises and register offices in England and Wales: the proportions of couples who marry away from home', *Population Trends* 107 (London: The Stationery Office, 2002), pp. 35–52.
5. House of Bishops, *Marriage: A Teaching document of the Church of England* (London: Church House Publishing, 1999), p. 8.
6. David Pailin, 'But who am I? The Question of the Theologian rather than the Question to the Theologian', in Mark Chapman (ed), *The Future of Liberal Theology* (Aldershot: Ashgate, 2002), p. 72.
7. In this regard it is interesting to note that it was as recently as 1991 that the House of Lords recognised the possibility of rape within marriage.
8. *Marriage and the Church's Task* (London: CIO, 1978), p. 33.
9. The situation regarding exclusivity is quite different; 61 per cent of those interviewed in 2000 believed that 'extramarital sex is "always wrong" ' a proportion which has increased slightly over the last two decades. Barlow et al, 2001.